Beyond Optimizing

Beyond Optimizing

• A Study of Rational Choice •

Michael Slote

Harvard University Press
Cambridge, Massachusetts
London, England
1989

Copyright © 1989 by the President and Fellows of Harvard College
All rights reserved
Printed in the United States of America
10   9   8   7   6   5   4   3   2   1

This book is printed on acid-free paper, and its binding materials
have been chosen for strength and durability.

Library of Congress Cataloging-in-Publication Data
Slote, Michael A.
  Beyond optimizing.

  Includes index.
  1. Ethics.   2. Choice (Psychology)   3. Reasoning.
I. Title.
BJ1031.S58   1989   170   88-24522
ISBN 0-674-06918-8 (lib. bdg. : alk. paper)

For Hans Kleinschmidt

Acknowledgments

Chapters 1 and 2 of this book derive from a set of Tanner Lectures that I gave at Stanford University in April 1985, and that were subsequently published under the title "Moderation, Rationality, and Virtue" in *The Tanner Lectures on Human Values,* vol. 8 (Salt Lake City: University of Utah Press, 1988). I would like to thank the Trustees of the Tanner Lectures on Human Values, a corporation, for permission to use some of this earlier material.

Chapter 5 makes use of material published under the title "Rational Dilemmas and Rational Supererogation" in a special issue of *Philosophical Topics* devoted to moral theory (14-2, Fall 1986). I would like to thank the editor for permission to make use of this earlier article in the present book, but it is worth pointing out that the article discussed a far more limited variety of possible self-regarding rational dilemmas than those considered here in Chapter 5.
All the putative examples of rational dilemma treated in the original article involve science-fictional situations where an agent has to choose among an infinite number of possibilities. But in addition to the infinitistic examples, the present book will propose and describe some far more homespun cases where an agent seems unable to make a rationally acceptable choice between two alternatives, and these more ordinary examples help to establish a wide-ranging analogy between the by-now familiar issues

Acknowledgments

surrounding the notion of moral dilemma and those arising in connection with the far less familiar idea of self-interested or self-regarding dilemma.

I am indebted to many people for helpful criticisms

I am indebted to many people for helpful criticisms and suggestions concerning earlier versions of the present work: among them Jonathan Adler, Michael Bratman, Stephen Braude, Earl Conee, Alan Donagan, Gail Fine, Jonathan Glover, Patricia Greenspan, Barbara Herman, Julius Moravcsik, Philip Pettit, Peter Railton, Don Regan, Georges Rey, Jean Roberts, Gregory Trianosky, and Tim Williamson. I have benefited greatly from Lindsay Waters's editorial suggestions, and I would especially like to thank Shelly Kagan and an anonymous referee for perceptive comments which led, at a crucial juncture, to major revisions.

My thanks also to Kathy Lossau and Linda Paul for help in proofreading and preparing the index, and to Lake Jagger for typing the manuscript.

Contents

It is important to realize that not even a first approximation of a comprehensive theory of strong interactions exists. We are therefore willing to settle for a much less ambitious goal, to push general symmetry arguments as far as possible. Success in this undertaking to date has been real, though limited.

Michael J. Longo
Fundamentals of Particle Physics

Introduction

Philosophy, economics, and decision theory have long been dominated by maximizing or optimizing models according to which rational choice—or at least self-interested rational choice—consists in seeking or achieving one's own greatest good or greatest preference-satisfaction. But in what follows I shall be arguing that our ordinary intuitive understanding of practical rationality is far more complexly contoured than anything suggested by these prevalent models, and also that maximizing/optimizing views of rational choice and action are insufficiently supported by the considerations and arguments typically offered in their favor. Theorists have long ignored or misunderstood our common-sense views about self-regarding rationality, but by exploring our intuitions about rational choice I hope to show that choosing what is best for oneself may well be neither a necessary nor a sufficient condition of acting rationally, even in situations where only the agent's good is at stake.

My description and evaluation of the common-sense alternative to optimizing and maximizing models takes its inspiration from the economists' notion of "satisficing," but gives that notion a distinctively philosophical elaboration that takes it and us far beyond where economists—and only some economists at that—have been willing to go. Defenders of satisficing claim that it sometimes makes sense not to pursue one's own greatest good or desire-fulfillment, but I think it can also be shown that it sometimes makes sense deliberately to reject what is *better* for oneself in favor of what is *good and sufficient* for one's purposes. Those who choose in this way demonstrate a modesty of desire, a kind of moderation, that seems intuitively understandable, and it is important to gain a better understanding of such moderation if we wish to become clear, or clearer, about common-sense, intuitive rationality.

For example, a normal, sensible individual may sometimes turn down an afternoon snack which he knows he could enjoy without spoiling his figure or his appetite for dinner; and it likewise makes sense for someone to desire, for instance, to be a really fine lawyer like her mother, but not desire to be as good a lawyer as she can possibly be. This limitation of ambition or aspiration may not stem from a belief that too much devotion to the law would damage other, more important parts of one's life. In certain moderate individuals, there may be limits to aspiration and desire that cannot be explained in optimizing terms, and in the earlier parts of this book I shall attempt both to show that such limitations are not obviously misguided and to indicate how rational moderation so conceived compares and contrasts with Epicurean, Aristotelian, and Christian views of moderation.

However, a fuller picture of common-sense rationality requires us to go beyond the topic of moderation to a consideration of the ways in which our intuitive picture of rational choice runs parallel to common-sense morality, as it has recently been described by philosophers. Much of recent moral philosophy has been dominated by a clash between common-sense or intuitive views about right and wrong and utilitarian or consequentialist views of right and wrong, and the former are in fact typically described and defended *by contrast with* the unified, simple picture of morality offered by the latter.

Standard consequentialism holds roughly that an action is right if and only if it leads, or is likely to lead, to overall results as good as those that would have come from any alternative action available to the agent. (The utilitarian holds, in addition, that happiness, or pleasure, or preference-satisfaction is the only thing that makes results good.) But common-sense morality diverges from this simple optimizing criterion of moral behavior in a number of notable ways. For example, it is presumably better that one innocent person die than that five such people should die. Yet where one can save five people from certain death only by killing some innocent bystander, such killing seems intuitively to be morally wrong or forbidden; and philosophers use the technical expression "deontological restriction" to designate this feature of common-sense morality—to designate, that is, the common assumption that the producing of overall good or best results is sometimes morally forbidden or restricted.

In addition, on many occasions in their lives people *might* wish to pursue the greatest good for all mankind, but because of the personal sacrifice that would be involved, such behavior seems heroic or especially praiseworthy, rather than obligatory. Utilitarian consequentialism requires us always to act for the greatest good of the greatest number, but in common-sense terms it may be morally permissible to focus more on one's own good than on the happiness of others. So those who give up their own projects, interests, and concerns to act for the greater good of mankind are ordinarily regarded as going beyond the dictates of duty—philosophers call this acting supererogatorily—but consequentialism, precisely because it insists that one do the best one can, leaves no room for moral supererogation: barring ties for first place, everything it morally permits it morally *requires*.

The main task of the present book will be to show that the principal features which distinguish common-sense or intuitive morality from (utilitarian) consequentialism have analogues in our ordinary understanding of rational self-regarding choice. And just as the common-sense view or "theory" of right and wrong is insightfully characterized in terms of the way it contrasts with consequentialist morality, so too, it will be seen, our intuitive view or theory of self-regarding rational choice is best described and understood by setting it in contrast with a maximizing/optimizing theory or model of rational choice. (In speaking of common-sense theory I mean nothing more tendentious than a view or amalgam of views whose merits and demerits are a proper subject for theoretical discussion.) Optimizing or maximizing theories of rational choice require an agent always to do what is likely to be best or most preference-satisfying for herself, and such a model clearly rules out the possibility of rational supererogation, that is, of going beyond the requirements of practical reason, as well as precluding rational restrictions on an individual's choice of what is best for her. However, our ordinary thinking about rationality is sometimes tolerant of less than rationally optimal choices and thereby treats optimal choices as supererogatory. And in appropriate circumstances, common-sense rationality also requires limits to be set on the pursuit and achievement of individual good. These claims may indeed at this point seem surprising and highly unmotivated, but I believe the examples that follow and the theoretical considerations urged and clarified along the way will demonstrate the abundant motivation and support that lies behind these initially implausible claims (they will seem most implausible, certainly, to those accustomed to theorizing on maximizing/optimizing assumptions).

Philosophers have long sought to base morality in views about practical reason, either by identifying what is right with the rational or by claiming that all distinctions of morality reduce to distinctions about our (rational) reasons for actions or choices. But philosophers have also been attracted to the idea of treating moral and rational distinctions as analogous, whatever the prospects of reducing the one group of notions to the other. Such a view leaves it open whether all moral claims and distinctions are ones which the agent has reason to act on, but for all that, the idea of a parallelism between rationality and morality has had an enormous appeal to philosophers and a great influence on recent ethical theory. The cumulative effect of *Beyond Optimizing* will be, I hope, to support and indicate some important implications of this powerful and influential idea of analogy between the rational and the moral.

Thus if I can demonstrate that our ordinary understanding of extramoral, self-regarding rationality diverges from optimizing views of rational choice in much the same way in which ordinary moral thinking diverges from standard optimizing consequentialism, the very fact of this analogy will do something—though just how much is not clear—to strengthen the case in favor of common-sense morality. Optimizing/maximizing rationality makes no allowance, for instance, for rational supererogation or for rational restrictions on the pursuit of personal good or preference satisfaction; hence, so long as we fail to recognize the possibility of any alternative view of rational choice, the idea of analogy between the moral and the rational exerts critical pressure against common-sense morality's supererogations and its deontological restrictions on pursuing overall (human) good. However, if I can show that there is a common-sense conception of rationality that allows for supererogation and imposes restrictions on personal optimizing/maximizing, then moral supererogation is correspondingly buttressed and the idea of moral restrictions on impersonal optimizing/maximizing— that is, on the pursuit of overall good—may be less problematic than it sometimes seems. Common-sense morality as a whole and in various of its parts receives some support, therefore, from the parallelism with the common-sense view of self-regarding rational choice.

At no point, however, shall I be opting for any particular moral theory or view of rational choice. I shall use the existence of a common-sense view of self-interested rational choice to support or discredit objections to common-sense morality, but it will also be clear that it doesn't discredit them all, and common sense generally is itself open to question on a number of grounds. The discussion will bring to light the existence of a common-sense rational analogue of common-sense morality and show more generally that we need not be slaves to received views of rational choice. But the common-sense view of rationality may or may not in the end be the best theory of rationality; it is, however, pervasive of our ordinary life and thought, and even if the interests of theory eventually take us away from this starting point and cause us to reject it, it is important to understand what we are rejecting and what, if we do so, we allow ourselves to lose.

On the other hand, standard optimizing and maximizing models of rational choice are called into question not only by the very existence of a widely divergent common-sense view of rationality, but also by the fact that they are underdetermined—that is, incompletely supported—by the best reasons that have been given in their favor. Unlike the richly structured common-sense view of rationality, optimizing and maximizing models are based on the idea that the rationality of choices depends solely on how (expectably) good or preference-satisfying their consequences are for the chooser. But this fundamental idea is also consistent with certain alternative models of rationality that I shall introduce and explore at some length later in the book. It will turn out, then, that in the theory of rational choice our options are far more numerous and difficult to evaluate than has previously been suspected. In fact, our problems about self-regarding rationality are every bit as challenging as those we face in moral theory.

· 1 ·

Moderation and Satisficing

It is widely assumed by philosophers (and of course others as well) that individualistic or extramoral practical rationality is subject to a condition of maximization: that the rational egoist, or the average non-egoist under conditions where the welfare of or commitments to others are not at issue, will seek to maximize her own good, or well-being. Utilitarians like Sidgwick and anti-utilitarians like Rawls both seem to assume that it is egoistically, individualistically, irrational not to maximize one's satisfactions and seek one's own greatest good.[1] More recently, however, some explicitly non-maximizing conceptions of personal well-being over time have been suggested by Amartya Sen and Charles Fried, who have, with differing degrees of vehemence, defended the notion that considerations of equality in the intertemporal distribution of goods in a single life have some independent weight in the reckoning of the goodness of lives.[2] The rational individual will wish to consider how much good for himself given courses of action will produce but also how evenly or equally the resultant good or satisfaction will be distributed across different times of his life, and he will allow for trade-offs between total amount of satisfaction and equality of distribution of satisfaction in deciding what courses of action to follow.

But even such non-maximizing conceptions of human

good and the rational planning of lives never suggest that the egoistic individual, or the non-egoistic individual in situations where only his own well-being is at issue, should ever do anything but optimize; what gives way in such conceptions is the idea that the course of action yielding the most good or satisfaction is always best for a given individual, but the assumption that the rational individual does the best he can for himself remains unscathed. Fried and Sen in effect tell us that human well-being must be more complexly reckoned than simple (or non-gimmicky) maximizing accounts permit, but they do not propose that the rational egoistic individual, in sometimes seeking *less than the most* available good or satisfaction for herself, might also seek what is *less than best* for herself (both at an isolated given time or over a lifetime). However, I want to argue for just this sort of possibility. In doing so, I know that I shall be defending views which, in the light of unbroken philosophical tradition, will at least initially seem bizarre and implausible. But I think a variety of examples drawn from ordinary life help to underscore the coherence and intuitive force of the idea that we may rationally seek less than the best for ourselves and sometimes even reject what is better for ourselves for what is good enough. However, a number of conceptual and other objections naturally arise in connection with these theses and I hope that by providing answers to those specific objections I may persuade you that we are not going to fall into conceptual confusion or contradiction by rejecting or questioning the view that individualistic rationality requires us to maximize or, more broadly, to optimize with respect to our own good.

I

The idea that a rational individual might seek less than the best for himself was originally developed, I believe, in the literature of economics. The term "satisficing" was coined for the discussion of such behavior, and I shall make use of the term here. What the economists have done, however, is point to an aspect of human behavior (both individually and in groups) that philosophers have traditionally ignored, and I shall be discussing and articulating the idea of satisficing in an attempt to give an adequate philosophical account of this phenomenon. The emphasis will be on conceptual and moral-psychological issues, rather than on the sort of technical economic-theoretic development of the notion of satisficing that can be found in the literature of economics.

Consider an example borrowed from economics.[3] An individual planning to move to a new location and having to sell his house may seek, not to maximize his profit on the house, not to get the best price for it he is likely to receive within some appropriate time period, but simply to obtain what he takes to be a good or satisfactory price. What he deems satisfactory may depend, among other things, on what he paid for the house, what houses cost in the place where he is relocating, and on what houses like his normally sell at. But given some notion of what would be a good or satisfactory price to sell at, he may fix the price of his house at that point, rather than attempting, by setting it somewhat higher, to do better than that or do the best he can. His reason for not setting the price higher will not, in that case, be some sort of anxiety about not being able to sell the house at all or some feeling that trying to do better would likely not be worth the effort of figuring out how to get a better price. Nor is he so rich that any extra money he received for the house would be practically meaningless in terms of marginal utility. Rather, he is a "satisficer" content with good enough and does not seek to maximize (optimize) his expectations. His desires, his needs, are moderate, and perhaps knowing this about himself, he may not be particularly interested in doing better for himself than he is likely to do by selling at a merely satisfactory price. If someone pointed out that it would be better for him to get more money, he would reply, not by disagreeing, but by pointing out that for him at least a good enough price is good enough.

Such a person apparently fails to exemplify the maximizing and optimizing model of individual rationality traditionally advocated by philosophers. But I think he nonetheless represents a possible idea of individual rationality, and much of the literature of economics treats such examples, both as regards individuals and as regards economic units like the firm, as exemplifying a form of rational behavior. Though one might hold on to an optimizing or maximizing model of rationality and regard satisficing examples as indications of the enormous prevalence of irrational human behavior, economists have not done so and I think philosophers would have even less reason to do so. For there are many other cases where satisficing intuitively seems rational, or at least not irrational, and although some of these are purely hypothetical, hypothetical examples are the stock-in-trade of ethical and moral-psychological theory even when they are of little or no interest to economists.

Imagine that it is midafternoon; you had a good lunch, and you are not now hungry; neither, on the other hand, are you sated. You would enjoy a candy bar or Coca-Cola, if you had one, and there is in fact, right next to your desk, a refrigerator stocked with such snacks and provided gratis by the company for which you work. Realizing all this, do you, then, necessarily take and consume a snack? If you do not, is that necessarily because you are afraid to spoil your dinner, because you are on a diet, or because you are too busy? I think not. You may simply not feel the need for any such snack. You turn down a good thing, a sure enjoyment, because you are perfectly satisfied as you are. Most of us are often in situations of this sort, and many of us would often do the same thing. We are not boundless optimizers or maximizers, but are sometimes (more) modest in our desires and needs. But such modesty, such moderation, is arguably neither irrational nor unreasonable on our part.

Of course, moderation has been exalted as a prime virtue in many religious and philosophical traditions. But when, for example, the Epicureans emphasized the rationality of moderation in the pursuit of pleasure, they recommended modesty in one's desires only as a means to an overall more pleasurable, or less unpleasant, life, and in the example mentioned above, moderation is not functioning as a means to greater overall satisfaction or pleasures. One is not worried about ruining one's figure or spoiling one's dinner, and the moderation exemplified is thus quite different from the instrumental virtue recommended by the Epicureans. The sort of moderation I am talking about, then, is not for the sake of anything else.

But then isn't the moderate individual who is content with less a kind of ascetic? Not necessarily. An ascetic is someone who, within certain limits, *minimizes* his enjoyments or satisfactions; he deliberately leaves himself with less, unsatisfied. The moderate individual, on the other hand, is someone content with (what he considers) a reasonable amount of enjoyment; he wants to be satisfied and up to a certain point he wants more enjoyments rather than fewer, to be better off rather than worse off; but there is a point beyond which he has no desire, and even refuses, to go. There is a space between asceticism and the attempt to maximize pleasure or enjoyment—do the best one can for oneself—a space occupied by the habit of moderation. And because such moderation is not a form of asceticism, it is difficult to see why it must count as irrational from the standpoint of egoistic or extra-moral individual rationality.[4]

Now the kind of example just mentioned differs from the case of house selling in being independent of any monetary transaction. But the example differs importantly in another way from examples of satisficing mentioned in the literature of economics. Economists who have advocated the model of rational satisficing for individuals, firms, or state bodies have pointed out that—quite independently of the costs of gaining further information or effecting new policies—an entrepreneur or firm may simply seek a satisfactory return on investment, a satisfactory share of the market, a satisfactory level of sales, rather than attempt to maximize or optimize under any of these headings. But this idea of rational satisficing implies only that individuals or firms *do not always seek* to optimize or are *satisfied* with attaining a certain "aspiration level" less than the best that might be envisaged. It does not imply that it could be rational actually to *reject* the better for the good enough in situations where both were available. In the example of house selling, the individual accepts less than he might well be able to get, but he doesn't accept a lower price when a higher bidder makes an equally firm offer. And writers on satisficing generally seem to hold that satisficing only makes sense as a habit of not seeking what is better or best, rather than as a habit of actually rejecting the better, when it is clearly available, for the good enough. Thus Herbert Simon develops the idea of aspiration level and of satisficing, but goes on to say that " when a firm has alternatives open to it that are at or above its aspiration level, it will choose the best of those known to be available."[5]

However, the example of the afternoon snack challenges the idea that the satisficing individual will never explicitly reject the better for the good enough. For the individual in question turns down an immediately available pleasure, something he knows he will enjoy. He isn't merely not trying for a maximum of enjoyments, but is explicitly rejecting such a maximum. (It may be easier to see the explicitness of the rejection if we change the example so that he is actually offered a snack by someone and replies: no thank you, I'm just fine as I am.) And I think that most of us would argue that there is nothing irrational here. Many of us, most of us, occasionally reject afternoon snacks, second cups of tea, and so on, not out of (unconscious) asceticism, but because (to some degree) we have a habit of moderation with regard to certain pleasures. The hypothetical example of the afternoon snack thus takes the idea of rational satisficing a step beyond where economists, to the best of my knowledge, have been willing to go.

At this point, however, it may be objected that the example may be one of rational behavior but is less than clear as an example of satisficing. The individual in question prefers not to have a certain enjoyment and certainly deliberately rejects the maximization of his enjoyments. But it is not clear that the moderate individual must think of himself as missing out on anything *good* when he forgoes the afternoon snack. For although he knows he would enjoy the snack, the very fact that he rejects such enjoyment might easily be taken as evidence that he doesn't in the circumstances regard such enjoyment as a good thing. In that case, he would be satisficing in terms of some quantitative notion of pleasure or enjoyment, but not with respect to some more refined or flexible notion of (his own) individual good, and the example would provide no counter-example to the idea that it is irrational to choose what is less good for oneself when something better is available.

But it would be a mistake to move too quickly in this direction. It is being granted—and how can it be denied?—that the person who turns down a snack would have enjoyed one. But doesn't that mean—in the circumstances as we have described them and barring irrelevant opportunity costs—that things would at least briefly have gone more enjoyably for him if he had taken a snack? If so, then in common-sense terms it seems undeniable that, in the short term, things would have gone at least slightly better for him if he had done so. (Or don't things go even slightly better with Coke?) However, even if the rejection of a snack does count as the rejection of a personal good—and of a personally better course of events—such facts may be obscured by the very smallness or triviality of the good in question. So it may be useful at this point to consider other examples, more purely hypothetical than the present one, where the good forgone through satisficing is larger and perhaps more obvious.

How do we react to fairy tales in which the hero or heroine, offered a single wish, asks for a pot of gold, for a million dollars, or, simply, for (enough money to enable) his family and himself to be comfortably well off for the rest of their lives? In each case the person asks for less than he might have asked for, but we are not typically struck by the thought that he was irrational to ask for less than he could have, and neither, in general, do the fairy tales themselves imply a criticism of this sort; so, given the tendency of such tales to be full of moralism about human folly, we have, I think, some evidence that such fairy-tale wishes need not be regarded as irrational. (In not regarding them as irrational, we need not be confusing what we know *about* fairy-tale wishes with what the individual *in* a given tale ought to know. In some fairy tales, people who ask for too much fail to get their wish or have it realized in an unacceptable way. But there is no reason to suppose that we consider the person who in a given fairy tale asks for enough to be comfortable not to be irrational, only because we mistakenly imagine him to have some evidence concerning the possible risks of asking for more than he does.)

Now the individual in the fairy tale who wishes for *less* than he could presumably exemplifies the sort of moderation discussed earlier. He may think that a pot of gold or enough money to live comfortably is all he needs to be satisfied, that anything more is of no particular importance to him. At the same time, however, he may realize (be willing to admit) that he could do better for himself by asking for more. He needn't imagine himself constitutionally incapable of benefiting from additional money or gold, for the idea that one will be happy, or satisfied, with a certain level of existence by no means precludes the thought (though it perhaps precludes *dwelling* on the thought) that one will not be as well off as one could be. It merely precludes the sense of wanting or needing more for oneself. Indeed the very fact that someone could actually explicitly wish (for enough money) to be comfortably well-off is itself sufficient evidence of what I am saying. Someone who makes such a wish clearly acknowledges the possibility of being better off and yet chooses—knowingly and in some sense deliberately—a lesser but personally satisfying degree of well-being. And it is precisely because the stakes are so large in such cases of wishing that they provide clearcut examples of presumably rational individual satisficing. But, again, the sort of satisficing involved is not (merely) the kind familiar in the economics literature where an individual seeks something other than optimum results, but a kind of satisficing that actually rejects the available better for the available good enough. Although the individual with the wish would be better off if he wished for more, he asks for less—we may suppose that if the wish grantor prods him by asking "are you sure you wouldn't like more (money or comfort or sheer felicity) than that?" he sticks with his original request. If we have any sympathy with the idea of moderation, of modesty, in one's desires, we shall have to grant that the satisficing individual who wishes for less is not irrational. Perhaps we ourselves would not be so easily satisfied in his circumstances, but that needn't make us think him irrational for being moderate in a way, or to a degree, that we are not.[6]

But at this point some doubt may remain about our description of the moderate individual's response to being granted a wish. It is not obvious that an individual who wishes for less than the most money (or comfort or well-being) he could ask for is satisficing in the strong sense defended earlier. He may make the seemingly modest wish he does because he is afraid of offending the wish grantor or in order to avoid being corrupted (or rendered blasé) by having too much wealth, and acting with such motives he will not exemplify the sort of satisficing moderation whose rationality I have tried to defend: he *will* be seeking what is best for himself under a refined conception of personal good that goes beyond mere wealth or material comfort.[7]

With this I can absolutely agree. An individual who asks for less than she could may indeed be motivated by factors of the above sort. My main point is, and has been, that there is no reason to insist or assume that such factors are always present when an individual asks for less than the most or best he can obtain. From the standpoint of the phenomenology of our own lives, it doesn't seem as if such factors are always present—we find it humanly understandable and not intuitively unreasonable that someone should lack an interest in the greatest heights of well-being or happiness and should actually reject the latter in favor of moderate or sufficient comfort or well-being. Why insist that some factors must always be present to turn putative cases of satisficing into cases, fundamentally, of optimization or maximization of the individual's (perceived) good?

The situation here resembles what is often said for and against psychological egoism. Many people—even philosophers—have argued as if it were practically a matter of definition that individuals seek their own greatest good, even when they appear to be sacrificing that good for the good of others. But nowadays philosophers at least seem to recognize that altruism and self-sacrifice cannot be ruled out a priori. Nonetheless, it in some sense remains empirically open that human altruism may turn out to be an illusion. It is conceivable, let us suppose, that a powerful enough psychological theory backing the universal selfishness of human behavior might eventually be adopted. But in the absence of such a theory, philosophers have been, I think, quite right to insist upon taking altruistic motivation seriously. Any moral psychology that wishes to remain true to our common or everyday understanding of things, to life as most of us seem to lead it, will assume that there is a phenomenon of altruistic motivation to explore and better understand, both conceptually and in its ethical ramifications.

Similar points can, I believe, be made about satisficing, or moderation in the sense delineated earlier. Some day economists and psychologists may show definitively that the best explanation of why humans act as they do requires us to assume that they are always maximizing or optimizing and thus that apparent examples of satisficing or moderation are illusory. But until and unless that happens, we should recognize—something philosophers have not previously noticed or admitted—that the common-sense understanding of our own lives leaves a definite recognizable place for occasional, perhaps even frequent, satisficing moderation. For in fact the phenomenon of moderation is not limited to fairy-tale examples, though I believe such examples allow one to see certain issues large enough and in sufficient isolation so as to make it easier to recognize moderation in the more muddied waters of everyday life. Even the example of the person selling a house need be altered only in minor ways in order to turn it from an example of not seeking the best for oneself into an example of actually rejecting the expectable better for the expectable good enough.

Imagine, for instance, that the person selling the house has a real-estate agent who has received a firm bid on the house that falls within the range the seller considers good enough. The agent tells the prospective buyer that it may take him three or four days to get in touch with the seller because he believes the latter is temporarily out of town; the buyer says he is in no hurry; in fact, the seller has not gone away and the agent conveys the bid to him on the same day it is made. The seller then tells the agent to let the prospective buyer know that his offer is acceptable, but the agent, who (we may assume) is not a satisficer, tells the seller that he really ought to wait a few days before accepting the offer that has been made. After all, he says, the offer is firm, and if you wait a few days before telling the prospective buyer that you agree to his terms, a better offer may come in.

Now in the circumstances as I have described them, the seller's likely benefit is greater if he waits—we are assuming that the seller is not rich, that the offer already made is firm, and that there is no reason to worry that the person who has made the offer may get cold feet (he doesn't expect his offer to be received for a couple of days). Yet the seller may tell the real-estate agent to convey his acceptance of the terms on offer without delay. Again, the reason may simply be that he considers the offer good enough and has no interest in seeing whether he can do better. His early agreement may not be due to undue anxiety about the firmness of the buyer's offer, or to a feeling that monetary transactions are unpleasant and to be got over as quickly as possible. He may simply be satisficing in the strong sense of the term. He may be moderate or modest in what he wants or feels he needs.

One cannot at this point reasonably reply that if the man doesn't want the (chance of) extra money for his house, then that cannot represent a good thing, a personal good that he gives up by immediately accepting the offer that has been made. An important distinction has to be made between what someone (most) wants and what advances his well-being (or represents a personal good for him). And, once again, a comparison with issues that arise in connection with altruism and moral behavior generally may help us to see the point. If altruism makes sense, then presumably so too does the notion of self-sacrifice. But the idea of deliberate self-sacrifice involves the assumption that what a person (most) wants need not be what advances his own personal well-being, what is (in one everyday sense) best for him. And this conceptual point carries over to discussions of moderation and satisficing. Just because the moderate individual asks for less money than he possibly could doesn't, for example, mean that additional wealth wouldn't be a good thing for him. The wishing and house-selling examples— as well as the earlier example of the rejected afternoon snack—indicate, instead, that an individual who does not want or care about a particular thing and who chooses not to have it, need not automatically regard that thing as not a personal good.[8] There is conceptual space for and human understandability in the idea of a personal good or element of one's own well-being that one simply doesn't care about or wish to have—and that one actually rejects—because one feels well enough off without it. It is a mere confusion, therefore, to say (as I have heard it said) that the person who turns down a certain good is nonetheless inevitably seeking her own good in some more refined sense, because she is maximizing the satisfaction of her weighted preferences on the whole, among which, after all, is presumably the preference not to have that unnecessary good (or the general preference not to have more than she needs). The same form of argument would be laughed out of court if applied in the area of morality and altruism: we all know by now that it would be absurd to argue that the individual who sacrifices his life for others must be seeking his own greatest good in doing so, because in doing so he is maximizing his weighted preferences, one very powerful one being the preference that he should die so others may live.[9] The only reason why a similar move is not instantly rejected in the area of individualistic rationality in connection with putative examples of moderation is that moderation as described earlier is a much neglected moral-psychological phenomenon. But once we get our sea legs on this topic, I think the sorts of objections to the phenomenon that naturally arise will be seen (at least in the cases mentioned above) to be as groundless as the sorts of objections to psychological altruism that abounded in earlier periods of philosophy but are now largely discredited.

On the other hand, once we become aware of the distinction

between seeking our own greatest good and attempting to maximize the fulfillment of our self-regarding preferences, we may seek to understand individualistic rationality solely in the latter terms. We may claim, that is, that an individual is self-regardingly rational if and only if she maximizes the expectable satisfaction of her (firm, consistent, transitive) self-regarding desires/preferences. Such a view would indeed allow us to regard satisficing moderation, as described above, as rational, since the moderate individual may firmly and consistently prefer to forgo certain personal goods, certain heights of well-being or happiness. But this understanding of practically individualistic rational choice nonetheless clashes with some of our most deep-seated ideas and intuitions about rational choice, and in the end is no more adequate to common-sense views of rationality than optimizing/maximizing views that focus on personal good.

The preference-maximizing standard of rationality—once it is clearly detached from the idea of optimizing the agent's own good—allows one to treat the moderate individual as rational, but it also forces one to regard the thoroughgoing non-instrumental ascetic as completely rational. The preference-maximizing model has no way of ruling out the possibility of an individual with a fundamental consistent preference (within limits dictated by health) for the least comfort, the fewest enjoyments; and yet because our ordinary thinking tends to assume a connection between self-regarding rationality and the agent's good, we naturally regard the ascetic (but not the moderate individual) as perversely, irrationally, *thwarting* his own good. So any attempt to cast maximizing rationality loose from agential good and conceive it entirely in terms of the maximization of whatever preferences the agent (fundamentally, consistently, and so on) has will be unable to capture some of our deepest common-sense intuitions about self-regarding rationality.[10] (Further reasons for this conclusion will emerge in subsequent chapters.)

II

Of course, we have also seen that optimizing/maximizing views of rationality that focus on the agent's good have difficulty accounting for our intuitions about satisficing moderation. But despite those intuitions, the defender of optimization can nonetheless argue in various ways for the irrationality of rejecting the personally better for the personally good and sufficient, or good enough. For example, in response to my account of satisficing moderation, Philip Pettit has claimed that the person who rejects what is better for himself in favor of what he considers good enough may have a reason for choosing what he chooses—what he chooses is, after all, good enough—but has no reason to choose what he chooses in preference to what he rejects. There may be a reason to wish for or choose moderate wealth or well-being, but there is no reason for the moderate individual I have described to choose moderate wealth or well-being over great wealth or well-being, and for that reason, according to Pettit, his choice counts as irrational or unreasonable.[11]

This objection, however, is extremely problematic. It is not, to begin with, a general condition of rationality that in choosing between two options one has a reason to choose one of those options rather than the other—otherwise, we would sometimes really be in the position of Buridan's ass. When two equally (or incommensurably) good or self-beneficial options present themselves, it need not be irrational to choose one of them, even though one has no reason to prefer it to the other. (I have somewhere read that Arthur Balfour once spent twenty minutes trying to decide whether there was any reason for him to go up a staircase to the left or one to the right in order to join a soirée to which he had been invited.) In the second place, reasons can be relative to an individual's concerns, her world view, or even her habits; and from the distinctive standpoint of the moderate individual, there may well be a reason to prefer moderate wealth (well-being) to great wealth (well-being). The fact that great wealth is much more than she needs (or cares about) can count, for such an individual, as a reason for rejecting great wealth and choosing moderate wealth, but of course such a reason will not motivate, or even occur to, someone who always seeks to optimize. The moderate individual will thus sometimes possess a statable reason for preferring what is less good for herself, but a reason precisely of a kind to lack appeal to the maximizing temperament.[12]

But this is not to claim that the moderate individual *always* chooses less than the best for himself. Other things being equal he will prefer what is better for himself to what is less good for himself; but from his particular standpoint, other things are not equal when what is less good for himself is good and sufficient for his purposes, and what is better for himself is much more than he needs or cares about. In such circumstances he can articulate a reason—a reason I think you and I can understand and empathize with—for choosing what is less good for himself. But faced, for example, with the choice between great wealth and dire poverty, he would have reason to choose the former (the moderate individual is not an ascetic) and indeed with respect to most choices between better and worse for himself he would (be able to) prefer the better-for-himself to the less-good-for-himself.

Moreover, although we have up till now been focusing on examples having to do with the appetites or material possessions, the idea of satisficing moderation has application to desires and projects that lie outside the pursuit of personal good or well-being narrowly conceived. Certain desires for achievement, such as the desire to solve a mathematical problem, may be neither morally motivated nor primarily focused on the good of the individual; but in some sense they are self-regarding (one doesn't simply desire that *someone* should solve the problem), and it is certainly possible to pursue such desires in a satisficing manner. One may have a personal ideal, such as the desire to be a really fine lawyer, without wishing to be better than other lawyers or the best lawyer possible or even the best lawyer it is possible for one to be. One's mother may have been an excellent lawyer, and one may simply want to emulate her. When asked "Don't you want to be the best lawyer you can possibly be?" one may reply "No, I just want to be a really fine lawyer, like my mother; I have no desire for anything beyond that," and this reply may express an inherently understandable compound of ambition and its limits, rather than a concern that too much devotion to the law might interfere with other, more important, life goals.

However, we are not yet quite out of the woods. We must consider a further objection to the rationality of satisficing moderation based on Donald Davidson's influential discussion of the notion of weakness of will. In his essay "How is Weakness of the Will Possible?" Davidson characterizes weakness of will, or incontinence, as involving, roughly, the intentional doing of some action x, when the agent believes that there is some available alternative action y which it would be better for him to do than to do x.[13] Davidson points out that the Aristotelian account of incontinence (sometimes) makes reference to the idea of an agent's going against some (prior) decision or choice, but Davidson wishes to allow us to speak of incontinence even when the agent who performs some act other than the one he judges to be best never actually decided or intended to do that best act, and he mentions passages in Aristotle that lend support to such an understanding of the concept of incontinence or weakness.

Now as we have seen, the moderate individual in a moment of moderate choice may choose an option that benefits him less, is less good for him than some alternative available in the circumstances. But if he chooses the less good option, does he not in fact fall under Davidson's seemingly reasonable definition of incontinence and thus automatically count as failing to act rationally?

I believe we have a confusion here, one that turns in part, but not entirely, on an ambiguity in the notion of an option. When we speak of an individual's deciding between options, the options spoken of may be certain choices, acts of choosing, or the assured results (assuming an absence of uncertainty) of those choices. In the situation where someone chooses between (having) great wealth and (having) moderate wealth, we can think of her options either as choosing great wealth versus choosing moderate wealth, or as having great wealth versus having moderate wealth, and small as this difference appears to be and in most circumstances actually is, the distinction is crucial to the existence or non-existence of incontinence in cases of satisficing moderation. Davidson (rightly) characterizes incontinence in terms of actions, not results of actions; it is only when we perform the less good action that weakness of will is said to be involved. But when the moderate individual chooses the option that is less good for herself in the sense that it involves her being less well off than she would be under some other option, we are comparing the results of certain choices. We are saying that (the act of) choosing moderate wealth will result in her being less well off than if she had chosen great wealth. Nothing has yet been said about the comparative merits of the choices themselves, in the sense of the acts of choice that are involved here. That is, we haven't yet said that *choice* of less is a worse act than *choice* of more, and a moderate individual will deny that. So the case doesn't fall under Davidson's description.

It is a mistake, therefore, to slide, in the way I illustrated earlier, from the claim that a certain option is less good for someone than some other to the claim that the first option is less good, and thence to the claim that the individual who takes the first option has acted incontinently in Davidson's sense. And if we distinguish between options as states of affairs that result from certain choices and options as choices (or acts of choosing), we shall be less likely to imagine that moderation involves weakness of will.

Of course, some philosophers—most notably G. E. Moore in *Principia Ethica*[14]—have assumed as obvious and even as definitional that it is always best to produce the best consequences one can. But deontological moral theories precisely deny this connection, and it gravely misconstrues the character of such theories to assume that they can be reformulated without alteration of content so as to advocate the production of best consequences suitably understood.[15] Since deontological theories are coherent, the connection between best action and action with (expectably) best results is neither self-evident nor, presumably, definitional; and in any event, it is even less plausible to maintain a tight connection between the best action an individual can perform and the action that benefits *him* most. Just as the individual who sacrifices her well-being for the benefit of others may coherently claim to have done the best she could, to have performed the best act available to her in the circumstances, there is no reason why a moderate individual who rejects dazzling levels of well-being for moderate contentment must hold that it would have been better for him to act otherwise. He has his reasons for rejecting, say, great wealth and there seems to be no reason why he should not be willing to stand by what he has done and hold (though he need not proclaim it from the rooftops) that he has done the right thing in the circumstances, given his own tastes and interests. He has done what he considers the best thing for him to do, even though he has not acted to insure his own highest or best level of well-being. Nothing seems to be amiss in what he has done, and there is no reason to suspect him of incontinence once we distinguish the evaluation of results from the evaluation of actions (including choices) and notice that the term "option" is ambiguous as between actions and results.[16]

★   ★   ★

Let me now conclude this first chapter by saying something about the directions in which our discussion of satisficing moderation can or will take us. The idea that self-seeking or self-regarding rationality may be moderate in its aims and intentions finds a notable parallel within the sphere of morality, which I want at this point briefly to outline.

If we can make sense of the idea of rationally seeking less than the best for ourselves, we can also make sense of a kind of "moral satisficing" that is in many ways (though not, as we begin seeing in Chapter 5, in all ways) analogous to individualistic satisficing. From the standpoint of common-sense *morality* it can be acceptable, permissible, to be less than optimifically benevolent or beneficent, to give others less than one is in a position to give them, so long as one is sufficiently beneficent, that is, gives others a good deal or enough. The following example should help to clarify what I mean:

The manager of a resort motel discovers, late one evening, that a car has broken down right outside the premises. In the car is a poor family of four who haven't the money to rent a cabin, but the manager has the power and authority to offer them a cabin gratis, and she in fact decides to do so. But in acting thus benevolently, she doesn't go through the complete list of all the empty cabins in order to put them in the best cabin available. She simply goes though the list of cabins till she finds one in good enough repair and large enough to suit the family. In fact, however, there is a better room free that she will easily find if she proceeds further through the list, but she chooses the cabin she does because it seems a satisfactory choice, good enough, not because she is an optimizer who thinks further search through the list of cabins will not be worth it in terms of time expended and the likelihood of finding a sufficiently better cabin.

In such circumstances optimizing act-consequentialism would presumably hold that she should look further, but I think ordinary morality would regard her actions as benevolent and not wrong. She has done well enough by the family in question and had no obligation to do better. But in addition to not requiring someone to optimize with respect to the good of others, ordinary morality also permits one deliberately to reject what would be better for others for what is good enough. Consider, for example, our earlier fairy tale altered so that only the well-being of others is at stake. A warrior has fought meritoriously and died in a good cause, and the gods wish to grant him a single wish for those he leaves behind, before he enters Paradise and ceases to be concerned with his former life. Presented with such an opportunity, may not the warrior wish for his family to be comfortably well off forever after? And will we from a common-sense standpoint consider him to have acted wrongly or non-benevolently toward his family because he (presumably knowingly) rejected an expectably better lot for them in favor of what was simply good enough? Surely not.

The examples of the warrior and the hotel manager not only offer a good illustration of the idea of satisficing benevolence (beneficence), but also help to make it clear that common-sense morality differs from standard optimizing consequentialism with regard to the morality of benevolence quite apart from issues concerning agent-relative moral restrictions or permissions. For example, the fairy-tale warrior's less than (expectably) optimific choice is not justified on grounds of the unreasonableness or unfairness of the personal sacrifice he would be required to make if he made some other choice. His situation involves no possible sacrifice of any kind. Nor need there be any deontological restrictions in play in that situation which make it commonsensically impermissible for him to give his family more than he in fact chooses to do. Ordinary morality permits one sometimes to do less than the most or best one can do for others as long as what one does produces a large or sufficient amount of good for others. And so from a common-sense standpoint, satisficing benevolence—a kind of moral satisficing—is justified quite apart from considerations of undue sacrifice or the possible transgression of deontological restrictions.[17]

However, if there is intuitive force to the idea that satisficing beneficence can be morally justified in its own right, and apart from any appeal to the moral considerations that distinguish common-sense morality from act-consequentialism, we need to consider the possibility that even act-consequentialism and act-utilitarianism may be properly formulated in satisficing terms. Act-consequentialism is typically presented as holding that the rightness of an act depends on whether it produces the impersonally best consequences its agent can, in the circumstances, produce, and as such it has been seen as a unitary moral conception by both advocates and critics. But the just stated thesis of act-consequentialism can in fact be broken down into a pair of claims that need not go together. The idea that the rightness of an act depends solely on (the goodness of) its overall consequences can be separated from the idea that such rightness depends on an act's having the overall best consequences producible in the circumstances; the second thesis entails the first, but not vice versa. In that case, it is not only natural, but from the standpoint of the present book terminologically useful, to extend current usage of act-consequentialism so as to include any view that ties the rightness of actions solely to the overall goodness of their consequences. And in the light of the above examples, therefore, it seems possible to maintain a form of (utilitarian) act-consequentialism according to which an act may be right in virtue of producing good enough consequences, even though better consequences could have been produced in the circumstances. (For present purposes, I don't think it is important to try to specify what counts as good enough or to distinguish between the expectably and the actually good enough.)

Such "satisficing" act-consequentialism is certainly not

much in evidence in the recent and past literature of utilitarian consequentialism, but as a matter of fact there have previously been forms of consequentialism, of act-utilitarianism, that qualify as satisficing by the above criterion. Thus the original formulation of Bentham's Principle of Utility (a formulation Bentham never explicitly rejected) says that it "approves or disapproves of every action whatsoever, according to the tendency which it appears to have to augment or diminish the happiness of the party whose interest is in question: or, what is the same thing in other words, to promote or to oppose that happiness."[18] Because an act may promote or augment people's happiness without doing so to the greatest extent possible in given circumstances, such a formulation of the Principle of Utility, whatever its merits or demerits, can be treated as an expression of satisficing act-consequentialism. And the same holds for the "negative utilitarianism" of Karl Popper according to which we have a duty to minimize suffering and evil, but no general duty to maximize human happiness. (Popper's defense of his view refers to the common-sense intuitions I mentioned above in pointing out the common-sense permissibility of moral satisficing, of satisficing benevolence/beneficence.) I don't want to enter into the comparative strengths and weaknesses of Popper's and other writers' forms of satisficing act-consequentialism.[19] But it should be clear that such consequentialism can be regarded as a form of act-consequentialism and that by allowing one to do less than the most good one can do, it allows for supererogation in a way optimizing act-consequentialism does not, but common-sense morality does.

Moreover—and this is closely connected with the last point—satisficing act-consequentialism yields many of the same results ordinary morality achieves by means of its agent-relative permissions to pursue one's own projects and concerns. Consider a doctor who takes a great personal interest in studying India's artistic and religious heritage and who has to decide between providing medical assistance to the sick and starving in India and doing so for people in some other part of the world. If (he knows that) he can do more overall good elsewhere, the received optimizing view requires him not to go to India, but a satisficing moral conception can permit him to go to India, and satisfy his interest in things Indian, as long as he does enough good as a doctor there. (His choice will be supererogatory if he sacrifices that interest in order to go where he can do more good.) So satisficing (act-)consequentialism allows us some leeway to do things which common-sense morality justifies in terms of agent-centered permissions, but optimizing (act-)consequentialism forbids. (How much leeway depends, again, on how much counts as good enough.) Hence, to the extent reconciliation with common-sense judgments about particular examples is an advantage for a form of consequentialism—consider how this has been thought to be a strength of rule-utilitarianism—satisficing act-consequentialism may have definite advantages over optimizing forms.[20]

Our common-sense intuitions about rationality treat some actions as rationally acceptable even though their consequences are less than the circumstantially best possible for their agents. And we have now seen how the idea of rational satisficing leads naturally to the idea of moral satisficing and to a form of (act-)consequentialism which allows an act to be morally acceptable even when some alternative to it would have overall better consequences. (Henceforward, "consequentialism" will mean "act-consequentialism" unless the context indicates otherwise.) But having said as much, I would like to return to the sphere of rational choice. Our earlier examples of satisficing moderation illustrate two fundamentally different kinds of reasons that may lie behind and motivate individual satisficing. From the standpoint of moderation, these reasons qualify or stand up against our (*ceteris paribus* or standing) reasons for seeking our own greater good, and this sort of complexity is a far cry from what we find in optimizing/maximizing models of rationality. The latter acknowledge only one sort of fundamental self-regarding reason for choice and action—the advancement of personal good or of desire/preference satisfaction, for instance,—and in the next chapter I will develop this fundamental difference between common-sense moderation and currently dominant optimizing/maximizing views of rationality. That train of thought leads to another issue, which has been almost palpably omitted from our previous discussion: the question whether moderation in our present sense represents any sort of virtue or admirable trait and the connected question whether the tendency, in extra-moral contexts, to optimize with regard to one's own well-being represents a desirable or an unfortunate habit of mind and action. Our treatment of these two questions in Chapter 2 will prepare the way for, and actually lead in to, a critical discussion, in Chapter 3, of *whether it is always rational to optimize.*

· 2 ·

*Moderation, Rationality,
and Virtue*

Until now I have used the expression "satisficing moderation"
to refer to a kind of moderation not engaged in for the sake of
an overall greater balance of satisfactions: a moderation, therefore, that occupies a sort of conceptual middle ground between asceticism for its own sake and the instrumental virtue
of moderation recommended by the Epicureans. But you will
also recall that satisficing moderation as I have understood it
goes considerably beyond the satisficing that has been defended by Herbert Simon and others in the literature of economics and elsewhere. The satisficing individual may not only
fail to seek the best results for himself, but may in certain
circumstances actually reject the better or best for the good
enough; and I have argued that there may be nothing irrational
about such a choice.

I

I would now like to discuss two quite different common-sense
reasons for satisficing moderation that can be elicited from our
previous examples. To begin with, someone who rejects what
is better for himself may feel that a certain option will give him
much more than he needs, and from the standpoint of a
genuinely moderate individual that will be a reason to reject

the option—at least when there is an alternative that provides him with what he feels he does need. A reluctance to go greatly beyond what one (feels one) needs is thus a mark of the moderate individual, the individual modest in her desires or wants, and, at the same time, a locus, for such an individual, of reasons for choosing less than the best for herself or failing to aim for such an optimum. Such reasons are familiar and understandable, though sometimes their expression is a bit more informal and colloquial than anything indicated earlier. If someone keeps pressing me to accept great wealth, lavish accommodation, or an extra dessert, and I, being a moderate individual, keep turning down these things, I may end up saying with some emphasis, in exasperation, "who needs it?" And that will be an expression of the kind of reason mentioned earlier, of the moderate individual's desire not to go way beyond what he actually needs.

Of course, if a host is pressing one to accept an extra dessert, good manners, if not on the host's part, then at least on the part of the guest, might dictate to the moderate individual that he simply accede and take the unwanted extra dessert, but if we imagine a situation where there is less reason to mask one's feelings by forms of politeness, the expression "who needs it?" seems precisely fitted to convey an exasperated reluctance to take much more than one needs, and a moderate individual will naturally express himself in this way either to himself or to others when such circumstances arise. But not just the moderate individual. We can, roughly, characterize the moderate individual as someone whose wants are more modest than those of others and who thus finds herself more frequently than most of us in a situation where she fails to seek or actually turns down good things. But the moderate individuals among us do not constitute some moral-psychologically isolated though understandable subpopulation of our species. Elements of moderation are to be found in most or almost all of us, and a full appreciation of the understandability of satisficing moderation requires us to see that this is so.[1] We all say things like "who needs it?" sometimes, and we all turn down afternoon snacks or second desserts or cups of tea on at least some occasions whose underlying circumstances are basically the same as those assumed in the examples mentioned earlier.[2]

In case, however, there are any lingering doubts about how an individual can (take herself to) have reason to reject something good on the grounds that she has no need for it, it may be helpful, at this point, to consider a case where lack of need is treated as a reason quite independently of any effect upon the individual's (or anyone else's) well-being. Why is it that if offered a choice between having one copy and having two copies of the morning paper gratis, many of us would prefer to take just one copy? Need it be because we don't want to deprive someone else of a copy or because it is harder to carry around and get rid of two copies of a newspaper? Surely there are circumstances where neither of these considerations, or anything similar, is relevant, but where, nonetheless, we would be inclined to take one copy rather than two.

But why should this be so? The obvious answer, not only in the light of what has already been said but also on grounds of sheer common sense, is that some of us are quite naturally reluctant to take more than we need, when we can have everything we need without doing so. One takes the single paper because it answers one's need for information; one has no need for two identical newspapers. (I am assuming that one is not worried about losing the single newspaper and that the difference between the chance of losing two and the chance of losing one is negligible.) But in the circumstances I have described one is equally well off with one newspaper or two, so if the absence of need moves one to reject the offer of two newspapers, it does so quite independently of any consideration of well-being and of the whole issue of optimizing or satisficing. This may help us to see that the fact that something is absolutely unnecessary or much more than one needs really is a reason for action and choice that has force and validity with most human beings—even people who are initially dubious about satisficing will presumably see the point of rejecting the offer of two copies of the morning paper.

However, it might be possible to grant rational status to total lack of need in cases of the sort I have just mentioned, while denying the rationality of satisficing moderation as described earlier. One might say that considerations of well-being are always lexically prior to considerations of non-need, so that the fact of non-need can be used to break ties in situations, like that of the morning newspaper, where one is (by hypothesis) equally well-off whichever way one chooses, but cannot overcome differences of well-being. The fact that a certain level of well-being or enjoyment is much more than one needs would then fail to justify rejecting such well-being or enjoyment in favor of what was (merely) good enough, and satisficing moderation as we have described it would remain an irrational phenomenon, despite the fact that the appeal to a lack of need can *sometimes* justify rejecting an alternative.

Such a move is highly reminiscent of the treatment of considerations of equality in Sidgwick's utilitarianism. As Rawls and others have noted,[3] Sidgwick allows considerations of equality to have an influence on moral choices only to break ties among choices with equally good (pleasant) consequences. Considerations of aggregate well-being are lexically prior to reasons of equality, and this in effect gives equality a minimal role in Sidgwick's theory, a role far less than defenders of the moral importance of equality would be willing to accept. It has always struck me, however, and I am sure this will also have occurred to others, that Sidgwick's compromise theory represents a somewhat unstable solution to the problem of giving adequate weight to considerations of aggregate welfare and equality within an acceptable total moral theory. Sidgwick's idea that equality has enough weight only to break ties seems to be an extraneous imposition, in the name of reconciliation with common-sense intuitions, upon an underlying utilitarian moral conception. Utilitarianism itself and what motivates it according to traditional conceptions can provide no source of support for an independent factor of equality even as a means of breaking ties. Consistent with the motivation underlying utilitarianism, then, it would seem more appropriate to say that equally felicific (optimific) acts are both entirely permissible and right, even if one of them tends toward more equality than the other, and indeed more recent versions of act-utilitarianism have tended to drop any suggestion that equality ought to be used to break ties. Either equality counts for nothing intrinsically in the moral assessment of actions, or it should have a weight far greater than that allowed it by Sidgwick.

My own feeling, for what it is worth, is that the situation with regard to lack of need is quite similar. If one really grants that the fact of not needing two newspapers can represent a sensible reason to take a single paper, then considerations of non-need have and must be admitted to have a force independent of considerations of greater or lesser well-being. But if they do, then in those numerous satisficing cases where those considerations at least *seem* to have force sufficient to overcome certain kinds of considerations of well-being, we have, I think, no reason to doubt that such force exists. If we grant the independent existence of reasons of non-need, it seems implausible and untrue to our own best sense of things to hold that such considerations have force enough only to break ties and can never stand up against considerations of well-being. So if one is willing to allow that non-need can function as a reason *independently* of well-being, as with our newspaper example, it should become easier to accept the idea that non-need can have force *against* the idea of well-being, and satisficing moderation may seem less perplexing and outré as a phenomenon.

We have so far been concentrating on a single kind of rationale that can lie behind and motivate satisficing moderation. But our examples in fact reveal another quite different kind of consideration that can motivate the moderate individual and each and everyone of us in our more moderate moments. In Chapter 1, in discussing the standpoint of someone who turns down an afternoon snack or an extra slice of cake, I characterized such an individual not only as feeling no need for some additional good thing, but also as feeling perfectly satisfied as she is. Lack of need, of course, is the sort of reason for satisficing we have just been describing in detail, but the idea that someone is perfectly satisfied as she is invokes a new sort of satisficing consideration that is worth examining. In the situation where one is being asked to choose between one and two newspapers, or between great and moderate wealth, there is no issue of retaining the status quo, either newspaperless or lacking wealth altogether; but in the case where one is offered but turns down an afternoon snack or a second dessert, retaining the status quo is a considered option and is actually preferred to a good-yielding change. And I believe such cases contain a distinctive common-sense reason for satisficing precisely in virtue of the fact that the status quo is involved as an option. The very fact that some satisfactory or satisfying state is the one actually enjoyed at a given time may at that time be thought to yield a reason for preferring to remain in that state rather than making some transition to a satisfactory alternative state, and a certain primacy of the actual may thus be part of what lies behind the rejection of a second dessert or afternoon snack. I only claim that it is *part* of the explanation, not *all* of it, since such examples also gain support from the fact that the individual involved feels no need for the dessert or snack. But the absence of need cannot, I think, be all that is involved in making the example intuitively plausible. An individual turning down a second dessert might idiomatically express himself by saying "No, thank you, I'm fine as I am," and such a remark implicitly refers not only to the absence of any felt need for an additional dessert but also to the acceptability of the status quo. However, other cases arise where the same idiomatic remark would be made, but where there was nothing either to be gained or lost by abandoning the status quo, and I believe such cases give the clearest indication of the independent status, as a reason, of the sheer fact of actual (present) satisfactoriness.

Consider another harmless example concerning newspapers. Imagine that you are staying at a hotel and are one morning reading one of the newspapers that hotel provides gratis to its guests. Imagine further that one of the hotel's employees, newly arrived on the job, is so nervous and so eager to please that he offers you a different copy of the same paper in exchange for the one you have. "Perhaps you'd rather have this copy of the paper instead, sir," he says. Let us imagine that it is perfectly clear that this other copy is in no way superior to the one you have, and also that you may not keep both copies—every available copy is needed for the use of the guests. We have a clear example of misplaced attentiveness and recognizing this, but not wanting to hurt the feelings of the overeager employee, you simply say: "No, thank you, I'm doing just fine with the copy I have."[4]

What will be the motivation for rejecting the offered paper? Surely not the energy it takes to switch papers—it also takes energy to turn the offer down and a quick comparison of energies expended is highly unlikely to lie behind the rejection. But neither, as in so many of our other examples, can the motivation derive from the fact that the newspaper offered in exchange is seen as much more than one really needs or cares about. We are supposing one does really want to have a paper. In the circumstances mentioned there can only be one reason for turning down the exchange, the fact that one is fine, or doing fine, *as one is*; and I believe that the motivating force of the status quo is clearly evidenced in the example just mentioned. But if the satisfactoriness of the status quo is a motivating factor in cases where the issue of going beyond what one needs is irrelevant, I see no reason to deny it a (reinforcing) role in those cases where the issue of need or lack of need is also present. The person who turns down an afternoon snack would seem to have two sorts of motivation for doing so: the fact that he doesn't particularly need or care about the snack in question; and the entirely satisfactory nature of his present state, of the status quo; and when someone uses an expression such as "I am perfectly satisfied as I am" to turn down such a snack, he invokes both of these factors.[5]

The structure of self-regarding reasons available to a moderate individual is clearly more complex than anything to be found within an optimizing or maximizing—whether good-maximizing or purely preference-maximizing—scheme of individualistic rational choice. In common-sense terms, the two sorts of reasons we have been discussing can qualify or restrict the standing reasons agents have for seeking their own (greatest or highest) good, whereas any maximizing or optimizing view, though it rides roughshod over the intuitions that support the rationality of satisficing moderation, admits only one fundamental kind of individualistic reason and therefore may be thought by its proponents to have an advantage of theoretical simplicity over our common-sense ideas about rational choice.[6] This difference in theoretical simplicity will appear all the greater after we consider, in later chapters, the full range of differences between common-sense and optimizing/maximizing views of rationality. But for the moment, I don't want to discuss the relative merits of these two radically different approaches to rational choice; my main purpose has been, rather, to point out how much richer our theoretical options in this area are than has previously been suggested. The rationality of non-instrumental satisficing moderation may be open to numerous doubts; but it involves no logical incoherence, and it has an intuitive viability that should make us take it seriously as a theoretical option.

This is a good point from which to begin a transition from the defense of our intuitive views about moderation to an attack, in particular, on the maximizing/optimizing models of extramoral rationality that have so long dominated our (theoretical) thinking. We have seen that common-sense rationality contains the means of self-defense against currently prevalent ideas about extramoral rational choice; but it is also capable of generating reasons for doubting, even denying, the validity of optimizing and maximizing views.

The process of casting doubt on these views will begin with a consideration, in common-sense terms, of whether the tendency to optimize may not be more of a vice than a virtue. (*Good*-maximizing is one particular form of the optimizing tendency, but I shall not explicitly focus on the notion of maximizing.) The widespread tendency to treat optimization and maximization as the only possible models of extramoral rational choice has blinded us, I think, to some negative features of the general tendency to seek the best one can for oneself, and once we recognize the intuitive rationality of satisficing, it also becomes easier to recognize the intuitively greater praiseworthiness of satisficing moderation as compared with any general disposition to optimize.

II

It has sometimes been pointed out that the optimizing tendency may be in some measure self-defeating. A person bent on eking out the most good he can in any given situation will take pains and suffer anxieties that a more casual individual will avoid, and it is hardly clear that the pains and anxieties will (on average) be compensated for by goods garnered through optimizing alertness and energy. Moreover, it may be a psychological truth that an optimizing individual, someone who always seeks to make the best of the situations she is in, will tend to be unhappy when things are not going well, that is, when she has to make the best of a bad situation; and the more moderate individual might, as a matter of empirical fact, be more likely to remain contented when things were not going well. But these points turn on psychological assumptions and contingencies which, though plausible, do not reflect our deepest intuitive reasons for questioning, and even deprecating, the optimizing temperament. (They also suggest arguments against the universal rationality of optimizing; but I want to delay all *rational* criticism of optimizing till the next chapter and to concentrate for the present on whether the optimizing tendency is a virtue or a defect of character.)

Consider, then, for example, how much more planful and self-conscious the continual optimizer must be in comparison with the satisficer who does not always aim for the best and who sometimes rejects the best or better for the good enough. The satisficer need not consider and compare as many possibilities as the optimizer—indeed, quite typically, the satisficer will pursue the first option he notices; if it seems reasonably satisfactory, he will not bother even to consider other possibilities. Now the optimizer will see such a failure to consider alternatives as an irrational, perhaps even a willful, refusal to consider one's own best interests; and from the standpoint of such interests, as they define the perspective of the optimizing individual, the satisficer does seem irrational. But we are not restricted, in considering the merits of optimization and satisficing, to the internal standpoint of the optimizer. Nothing dictates its preferred or preferable status as a reference point for evaluation. We should also be interested, perhaps even be primarily interested, in how optimization can be seen and understood from a more impersonal perspective, most particularly, in how the optimizer *looks to others*.

Planning, self-consciousness, circumspection are all (noncontingent) enemies of spontaneity and of an adventurousness that most of us think well of, even admire. Prudence and long-range life plans, for example, have sometimes been granted the status of virtues in almost grudging, and certainly in lukewarm, terms, and the reason has typically been a countervailing valuing of the spontaneity and boldness that on purely conceptual grounds must be missing from the life governed by prudence and life-planning.[7] Optimizing at given different times need not, I suppose, involve any sort of spelled-out life plan nor even the playing-it-safe so characteristic of prudence in the ordinary sense. But the habit of optimizing does share the aspect of unspontaneous and constrained living that is characteristic of these other traits, and it is in all these cases a conceptual fact, not an accidental psychological generalization, that these negative features should attach to what are sometimes presumed to be virtues. To some extent we feel sorry for, think less well of, someone lacking in spontaneity, and the optimizing individual, who lacks spontaneity in a very high degree, can hardly seem admirable when regarded under that aspect. But that is not all.

The optimizing person has other negative features that further serve to undercut our antecedent sense that optimizing rationality is a desirable or admirable human trait. The optimizing individual—again, as a matter of conceptual necessity, not of accidental psychology—seems lacking in self-sufficiency. Now self-sufficiency as I shall be describing it is a much ignored trait, partly, I think, because the claims of self-sufficiency were so thoroughly overemphasized and exaggerated by philosophers in the ancient world. The Stoics in particular exalted self-sufficiency, *autarkeia*, to the status of an absolute and practically exclusive standard for evaluating human good and virtue, and we have every reason to shy away from their excesses. For the Stoic, the wise man or sage would be absolutely self-sufficient in his well-being, depending neither on loved ones nor on the fortunes of this world for his ultimate happiness. Nothing subject to loss or risk can feature in such a conception of happiness. But the Stoic ideal is not ours, and we have grown wary, and more than wary, of attempts to seal off human excellence or well-being from the risks and taints of the world, and of our less-than-ideal human nature.[8] We are very much in danger, as a result, of failing to recognize elements in the Stoic ideal that touch us very deeply and cannot be characterized as some sort of neurotic attempt to make human life absolutely safe. The ideal of self-sufficiency need not be carried to Stoic extremes, and indeed the notion has great currency in ordinary thinking about the world. We value, we admire self-sufficiency in the ordinary sense of the term, and a soberer ideal of such self-sufficiency can in fact be used as a touchstone for the criticism of optimization.

Consider, again, how the optimizer appears to others. Will not his tendency to eke out the most or best he can in every situation strike someone who witnesses or hears about it as lacking in self-sufficiency? Will not the optimizer appear needy and grasping and his persistent efforts a form, practically, of desperation, by contrast with the satisficer who accepts the good enough when he gets it?[9] Modesty in one's desires and needs is, and is as a matter of conceptual fact, an expression of self-sufficiency as ordinarily understood. A person eager for and intent upon the best (for himself) automatically appears (other things being equal) less self-sufficient than a person satisfied with less than the best, and so I am saying, among other things, that there is an inherent connection between aiming for what one takes to be sufficient, rather than for what is best, and a kind of personal self-sufficiency that most of us think well of.[10] To the extent the optimizer thus seems needy and somewhat desperate, as well as cramped and unspontaneous, we shall feel sorry for him and find it difficult, if not impossible, to think well of him. The habit of optimization will then be seen as an anti-virtue, an unfortunate and lamentable human character trait, and the habit of moderation regarded as a desirable trait, a (non-moral) virtue—a minor virtue perhaps, not the most admirable trait known to man, but a trait, nonetheless, in whose absence a human being becomes somewhat unfortunate and pitiable.

It is worth going back and considering how we have managed to reach this conclusion—I am sure those initially in favor of optimizing will suspect some sleight of hand or fallacy in the argument. We have arrived at the above (re)evaluation of the merits of optimization and satisficing moderation by deliberately refusing to judge the issue from the standpoint of the optimizing rational (and I have not questioned his rationality) individual. From such a standpoint optimizing choice must invariably seem not only rational, but ideal, and the "strategy" (as the optimizer might put it) of the satisficer irrational, pathetic, absurd. After all, from the optimizer's standpoint (and barring all moral issues for the limited purposes of this discussion) the whole point of action is to serve one's own interests and well-being, and for the optimizer it must seem self-evident that such an aim involves serving those interests, that well-being, to the greatest extent possible. It is only when one gets outside the optimizer's way of seeing things and tries to empathize with the satisficing temperament—seeing things from the satisficer's standpoint—that one may begin to recognize that optimizing is not an inevitable or inescapable human tendency. Once satisficing is understood sympathetically, we have the wherewithal to take a disinterested or objective look at the underlying personality structure or character of both the optimizing and the satisficing individual. And, as we have seen, a comparison of these two ideal types enables us to recognize some commendable features the satisficer possesses but the optimizer lacks.

III

It is worth noticing, at this point, that there is something cramped or constrained not only, as we have seen, about the tendency to optimize, but also about an exclusive concern with one's own interests and well-being. Like the optimizing individual, the egoist will appear lacking in self-sufficiency—as Nietzsche reminds us, benevolence toward others is a characteristic expression of a sense of satisfaction with oneself or with what one has; the ungenerous individual conveys an unavoidable appearance (relative, at least, to any recognizably human psychology) of dissatisfaction and insufficiency. So at least some of the reasons for our low opinion of egoistic individuals—the reasons deriving less from our moral and altruistic feelings and more from our sense of what is properly and self-respectingly human—mirror our earlier criticisms of the optimizing temperament, and I believe the interplay and analogy between what philosophers find it natural to say about the opposition between egoism and altruism and what I have here suggested about the opposition between moderation and optimization may help to clarify and support the picture I have been offering.

Both altruism and moderation are traits requiring cultivation. In some sense they do not come naturally, and parents, teachers, and others have a difficult task on their hands when they attempt to overcome or mitigate children's insatiable selfishness and greed. The typical simplified picture of how a child develops intrinsic concern for others involves the assumption that children need to go through an intermediate stage where they see a concern for others as furthering their own interests, and a similarly simplified picture of the attenuation of childhood demandingness and greediness might well depict the child as having to go through a stage where moderation was seen (in the Epicurean manner) merely as a means to greater overall satisfaction (the cake will spoil your dinner or give you a tummy ache). But just as the development of some degree of intrinsic concern for others is typically regarded as a form of moral progress, I believe that the development of some degree of non-instrumental moderation may also be good thing, a kind of human progress.

In comparing the satisficing and optimizing tendencies, I have not yet said anything specifically about the rationality of optimizing choice. But our remarks on the intuitive unattractiveness and deplorability of (constant) individualistic optimizing in fact help to clear the way for an argument against the universal rationality of optimizing: they may at the very least predispose us to take such an argument more seriously than we otherwise might. I shall be examining such an argument in Chapter 3, but the discussion of what is (from a common-sense standpoint) rationally criticizable in a tendency to optimize needs to be embedded in a larger context. We have seen that satisficing moderation tends to justify itself in terms of reasons such as "that is much more than I need" and "I am doing fine as I am." Such reasons are self-regarding and not moral. Yet neither are they purely instrumentalist in the sense of treating better results as always preferable. The reasons commonsensically invoked in favor of non-instrumental moderation are sui generis or at least not familiar from the recent literature of ethics.[11]

And beginning in Chapter 3, I shall be arguing that the self-regarding common-sense reasons we have mentioned thus far are only a few among a great variety of such reasons, differing from self-regarding consequentialist reasons in much the same way certain common-sense *moral* considerations differ from the moral considerations that traditional act-utilitarianism and act-consequentialism find acceptable. Among the most important of these, we shall see, are certain common-sense *rational restrictions* on individual optimizing.

· 3 ·

Rational Restrictions on Optimizing

I believe that the practically universal agreement among philosophers, decision theorists, and economists on the optimizing or maximizing character of (individualistic) rational choice has unduly limited our theoretical options, and that the possibilities in the area of practical rationality are at least as rich as the long-standing debate between common-sense morality and consequentialism shows morality to be. In moral theory we are faced with important and difficult questions concerning the respective merits of act-consequentialism and intuitive "ordinary" morality. And in the area of rational choice and action, I hope to show a fundamental divergence and disagreement between optimizing or maximizing models of practical rationality and an intuitive common-sense view of practical reason whose very existence has been obscured—for theorists at least—by their reliance on such models. It has also been widely assumed that some sort of optimizing or maximizing view is at least implicit in ordinary thought and practice, but we have already seen that this cannot be the entire picture: by our common lights optimizing with respect to one's own good is not necessary to rationality and maximizing one's expectable preference-satisfaction is not a sufficient condition of rational choice. And it turns out, in fact, that our common-sense view, or "theory," of rational choice bears to the (personally) optimizing view of rationality a relationship quite analogous to that which common-sense morality bears to impersonally optimizing consequentialism.

In the next four chapters, I shall be attempting to make good on that claim by discussing the particular, and possibly surprising, ways in which ordinary ideas about rational choice resemble those two aspects of common-sense morality in virtue of which it most familiarly and famously differs from act-consequentialism: namely, its deontological restrictions on impersonal optimizing and its permissions for the non-optimific pursuit of personal projects and concerns. The parallelism thus unearthed and explored will then enable the defender of common-sense morality to deny the long-standing charge that she must treat morality disanalogously from individual practical rationality. Rather, a common-sense view of morality most naturally goes with a common-sense picture of individualistic rational choice, and the two together naturally stand opposed to act-consequentialism (in morality) combined with the optimizing theory of individualistic rationality that so many philosophers have treated as the sole viable possibility in rational choice theory.

Our discussion will attempt to elucidate the character of common-sense rationality by describing its structural similarities to common-sense morality. But nowadays common-sense morality is itself most typically characterized by *contrast with* impersonally optimizing act-consequentialism (see the permissions and deontological restrictions mentioned just above). And given the natural analogy between impersonal good and personal good, it therefore seems reasonable to describe common-sense rationality by specifying the ways it deviates or differs from a personal-good-optimizing view of individualistic rationality. The parallelism between common-sense rationality and common-sense morality is thus demonstrated by showing that the former differs from the personally optimizing view of rationality in ways substantially analogous to the ways in which common-sense morality diverges from impersonally optimizing act-consequentialism.

Note, however, that this way of revealing and characterizing our ordinary thinking about practical rationality leaves to one side the preference-fulfillment-maximizing conception of rationality that is so prevalent among economists and decision theorists. But as I shall attempt to make clear in what follows, many points of contrast between ordinary practical rationality and the good-optimizing view also hold between the former and the preference model of rationality, and I shall also indicate where claims made in connection with the good-optimizing model of rationality cannot be made or need considerable transformation in order to be made in connection with the preference view. In the next four chapters our pursuit of analogy between common-sense morality and common-sense rationality will make it useful to focus primarily on the personal-good-optimizing conception of rationality, but the preference view is simply too important to neglect.

I

The feature of common-sense morality that has been most heatedly discussed in the recent literature of ethics, and that represents its sorest point of disagreement with act-consequentialism, is its commitment to deontological restrictions. The traditional concern with the way our ordinary obligations not to treat others badly limit the pursuit of self-interest has given way, in recent discussions, to an emphasis on the limitations such obligations impose on the individual's pursuit of overall, impersonal good: the common-sense obligation not to deceive or to harm (in most cases) regards it as wrong to deceive or harm someone even if by doing so one can make things on the whole better (for people) than by not doing so. Some highly controversial theoretical and moral aspects of our common-sense deontological restrictions have been brought to light in recent years, and I believe any attempt to show that there exists a common-sense understanding of extramoral rational choice running parallel to common-sense morality, and standing to the optimizing view of rationality in a relation similar to that which common-sense morality bears to standard act-consequentialism, must seek to convince us that there are common-sense rational restrictions on the pursuit of self-interest. It must point out some specific ways in which an individual's attempt to optimize (or maximize) with respect to her own good or well-being may sometimes be considered irrational; and in fact, two kinds of rational restrictions on optimizing can be elicited from our intuitive judgments about what is or is not rational. Before I can begin with the more controversial, but also more interesting, of the two, we need to take stock of the results of the past two chapters.

The idea of a common-sense approach to, or theory of, practical rationality running parallel to common-sense morality involves questioning the optimizing view, and I have questioned the received view by raising doubts about whether rational choice must be understood as always involving optimizing. But the idea that it can be rational not to optimize and the idea that optimizing is an anti-virtue do not obviously entail that there is anything *irrational* in a tendency always to make optimizing choices, though they certainly move us in that direction. It is important, however, to recognize some of the limits on what we have shown and can show. We have seen that a moderate individual may be satisfied with a certain level of enjoyment or well-being without believing herself to be as well off in the relevant respects as she could (hope or try to) be. All that is required is that she not want any more or better than she has, and it does not offend common sense to suppose that it is not irrational to have one's wants limited in this way. A person's desires (and hopes) may simply not extend to all possible (acknowledged) elements or levels of his well-being: he may be indifferent to what he would, if asked, acknowledge to be personal goods, things that would make his day or his life go (even) better. And in common-sense terms there may be nothing irrational here, if the person justifiably feels he is doing fine as he is, without those goods.

Such an attitude—with appropriate attendant behavior—is most noticeable and most frequent in individuals we call moderate, or modest in their desires. The capacity of such people for enjoying or benefiting from things need not be radically different from that of other people; rather, it is in how they pursue their own good that they differ from the non-moderate. Basically, the person who is modest in his desires doesn't seek to have more than he feels he needs (in order to be comfortably well off or to be doing well). And if the point at which such a person considers himself well enough off and is satisfied seems to us to be genuinely satisfactory, if the person doesn't seem to us to be under a delusion in thinking that he is doing well, then even those of us who are not particularly moderate would typically not regard him as irrational for not pursuing higher levels of personal good or enjoyment. We may even admire the moderate individual's independence of life's goods, his self-sufficiency.

Of course, the ascetic is also independent of the good things of life—can we come to grips with the ascetic's viewpoint unless we assume that what she insists on denying herself are things she herself finds good and enjoyable? But as I remarked earlier, most of us regard the ascetic's self-denial as perverse, a form of folly, in a way that it would ordinarily never occur to us to think of individual moderation.[1] In that case, if it seems intuitively that moderation as we have described it is not irrational, does that mean it is irrational not to be moderate, to want considerably more than one needs? I think not.

Most of us would find nothing rationally unacceptable, for example, in the attitude of someone who saw that a given item or episode was more than he needed, but thought that he would be better off for having it and that things wouldn't be entirely satisfactory until he did. Nor would we question the attitude of someone who thought she was doing just fine, but nevertheless felt there were certain good things she wanted to have (or enjoy or be) and wouldn't be entirely satisfied without. Such people do not, intuitively, seem irrational, greedy, or compulsive; many of us would recognize ourselves in the above descriptions. But neither, of course, are they particularly moderate. And to that extent common-sense views about the rationality of moderation differ from the Aristotelian conception of moderation or temperance. For according to Aristotle temperance or moderation is a habit of "medial" choice and desire with respect to bodily pleasures, and in every relevant situation the amount of food (or whatever) one should take is uniquely dictated by practical reason. By contrast, our present-day common-sense views are far more tolerant of diversity, and it would seem that both noninstrumental moderation and a desire for more or better than moderation (in the ordinary sense) would allow, can count as rationally acceptable in common-sense terms.[2]

Nevertheless, some instances of the general tendency to optimize may plausibly be regarded as irrational, and I think we are now in a position to see why. Our rational toleration for moderation is limited at the one extreme by a strong feeling that non-instrumental asceticism (or a despairing, bathetic view of our needs, of what is enough) is not a rational attitude toward one's own good. But at the other extreme there are also limits on what makes sense to us in the pursuit of individual well-being, self-interest, or enjoyment. It may not seem irrational to us for an individual to seek more than he needs, or not to be entirely satisfied with merely doing fine or being comfortably well off, but I think our rational toleration wears thin if there is no point (less than the best or most that could be desired or hoped for) at which such an individual would stop, be satisfied. With respect to various areas of human good our full rational toleration is extended only to those who at some point are willing to limit their pursuit of the good, to satisfice, and any person who finds nothing satisfactory less than the most or best she could hope or try for will inevitably appear greedy, compulsive, insatiable—in a word, irrational. So at one end asceticism and at the other a limitless pursuit of one's own good or self-interest are both rationally criticizable from a common-sense standpoint.[3]

I am saying, then, that the disposition to satisfice, to remain content with some perfectly satisfactory level less than the best possible, is widely regarded as a necessary condition of full practical rationality: those who pursue their own self-interest insatiably, who always optimize, seem to that extent irrational to our ordinary ways of thinking. And in that case there are common-sense rational restrictions on extramoral individual optimizing, on the individual's pursuit of her own good. Just as, from the standpoint of common-sense morality, there can be occasions when it is wrong to advance overall impersonal good, there are times when it is commonsensically irrational to act in such a way as to best advance one's own good or well-being. In case what I have in mind here is not yet entirely clear, let me illustrate the idea of rational restrictions with an example or two.

Imagine an individual who has frequently moved. Each house he has lived in has been satisfactory in many respects, but unsatisfactory in others. One had a porch and garden, but too little light; another had an attractive study—but one had to climb three flights of stairs to get to it; and so on. Let us assume, however, that the man finally moves into a house with all the features he has always wanted. Nothing about the house displeases him, except for one thing: he is sure it isn't the best house imaginable, and he is inclined to believe there may be better houses available in the great metropolitan area where he lives. And so with this thought in mind, he ransacks the housing advertisements in the local newspapers to see whether he can find something better than the house he is now in. I think most of us would regard this man's behavior and attitude as in some way irrational—as demonstrating a perverse or compulsive desire for home improvement.

The man's belief that better houses are possible is not, presumably, at fault: the idea of a best possible house is probably incoherent, and if it isn't, there is no reason to think our civilization has achieved its realization. So let us grant the man is correct in assuming that better houses may well be available in his area. And let us not deny that the man would benefit from the acquisition of a better house. Still something seems wrong.

The fact that one's situation could possibly be improved does not show that it is in any way unsatisfactory, and a house may be entirely (or thoroughly) satisfactory, even if a better may be available. Our notion of the entirely satisfactory is not a notion of perfection or (ideal) optimality: "perfectly satisfactory" does not entail "perfect."[4] And this distinction is built deeply into our ordinary thinking about human happiness and rational choice or desire. With respect to various familiar rubrics of human well-being or good, we believe things can be entirely satisfactory without being as good as one might hope for or desire. But it also seems true by definition that one (rationally) ought to be entirely satisfied with things as they are, when things as they are are entirely satisfactory and, further, that when one is entirely satisfied with things, one doesn't try for better (want to be better off). The upshot of these definitions, together with the common-sense distinction between the entirely satisfactory and the best possible, is a rational restriction on the pursuit of the good, an insistence that it is sometimes, or often, irrational to pursue or deliberately advance one's own well-being, good, pleasure.[5] But however intuitive such a restriction may seem, its very existence has been obscured by certain long-standing philosophical preoccupations. Philosophers interested in practical reason have focused on the good or the best life or on happiness *tout court*, or on pleasures and satisfactions (of desire), at the expense of such related notions as satisfactoriness and being happy or satisfied *with* one's (evolving) situation. But attention to the latter is precisely what is needed to bring our common-sense rational restrictions on optimizing into view. At this point a number of questions and objections may be raised, and in order to deal with them, it will be helpful to return to our example of the person seeking a better house.

Let us assume that the person who ransacks the newspapers every day looking for a better house cannot find anything unsatisfactory with the house he is in. To that extent it will seem to most of us irrational for him to be searching for a better house and not to be satisfied with what he has. And if we believe, further, that no house (short of the best conceivable) would entirely satisfy him, we shall think of his irrationality under the more particular rubrics of compulsiveness and insatiability. (I am assuming in our example that the man isn't pursuing better and better houses for reasons of conspicuous consumption, to keep up with the Joneses; it is only himself that he is seeking, but unable entirely, to satisfy.) Of course, we can imagine the man claiming that his present house is not entirely satisfactory precisely because a better one might be imagined (hoped for). But such a remark would sound very odd, and the oddness would result from its conflation here of the entirely satisfactory and the best possible. To treat such ideal conditions as necessary to thoroughgoing satisfactoriness in this area is offensive to our ordinary intuitions, and indeed, from the common-sense standpoint, it may be as much an error to pitch the standard of complete satisfactoriness too high as to set it—out of despair, bathos, or a lack of pride—too low.[6]

However, it might be said to be a mistake to treat the present example as an instance of our common-sense rational restrictions on optimizing, because the man who seeks a better house, if irrational at all, is irrational for *failing* to optimize.

The chance of finding and living in a better house is probably just not worth the labor involved in research, when one's present house is in every way satisfactory. So if the man searches, it must be through some sort of weakness of will or, more likely, an improper assessment of what is actually best for him; he will be irrational for reasons quite different from what was suggested above.

But how can we be so confident a priori that the chance of a better house is not worth the search? Even assuming that a law of diminishing returns applies, the man will presumably derive greater enjoyment or interest from a better house (a house he would consider better), and that differential would presumably extend over an extended period of time (it makes no difference to the argument that he might later seek an even better house). Moreover, the man may actually enjoy searching for a better house—the pleasure of the chase—so it isn't easy to justify the assumption that the man is not optimizing. And, perhaps more important, there is no reason to think that those of us who find his behavior irrational are implicitly *assuming* that he is not optimizing, that the effort to find a new house won't (expectably) make him better off. What from an intuitive standpoint seems criticizable in the man's attitude and behavior is not his misguided view of when he is likely to be better off, but rather his insistence on improving his condition, on achieving greater heights of well-being, when his situation is in the relevant respects entirely satisfactory as it is. What most immediately strikes us as irrational about him is his need to do (what actually may be) better and better for himself, his failure to recognize, in practical terms, when enough is enough. And so I believe it is as an illustration of rationally forbidden or unacceptable optimizing that our example of the man seeking a better house meshes with ordinary thinking about what is or is not rational.

However, we could face another possible objection to this way of viewing things. For it might be claimed that the individual who seeks a better house shows himself not to be entirely happy or satisfied with the house he has and so must experience a form of unhappiness or unpleasantness that someone satisfied with his house would not feel. Such a person thus ends up expectably worse off than he could be, because he makes efforts and suffers an unpleasantness that would be avoided if he were entirely content with the house he has. Again, he is irrational through a failure to optimize.

This objection suffers from mistakes we have previously mentioned, but has some interesting faults of its own. Why assume that contentment with his present house is really an option for the man? Why assume a priori that (people tend to assume a priori that) the unpleasantness of desiring another house together with his efforts to find a new house outweigh the prospects of finding such a house?[7] Indeed, why even assume that (people tend to assume that) it is unpleasant to want a different house from the house one has? True, the man who wants a better house is in a perfectly ordinary sense not entirely satisfied or happy *with* his present house. But as I mentioned above, this is a somewhat different concept from happiness *tout court* and from pleasure or the absence of un-pleasantness. May it not be possible to want things to change, and in that measure not to be happy with the status quo, yet to be happy with the way things are changing and are likely to change in the future?

According to Rawls, "A person is happy . . . during those periods when he is successfully carrying through a rational plan and he is with reason confident that his efforts will come to fruition."[8] And on such a conception, since plans typically involve changes from the status quo, a person may be happy at times when, assuming her desire and intention to fulfill the plan, she is not happy with things as they are. Nothing we have said about the individual seeking a better house rules out the possibility that his search is part of a life plan that sets the finding of better and better houses ad indefinitum as one of its (irrational) goals. I see no reason, then, to hold that such a person will necessarily find it unpleasant to desire, or be unhappy in desiring, a better house, even though he is not happy *with* his present house—or with his total present circumstances. During the periods when he happy with the way things are developing, with his life prospects, he is happy *tout court* precisely, in part, because he knows the status quo is not fixed and can be altered in accordance with plans of his own making. But it is easy to miss this point because of the fine distinctions it requires us to make. (Indeed, we have problems here not only because terms like "happy" can be involved in different expressions with different conditions of application, but also because one and the same phrase is subject to ambiguity: "he is happy as he is" can be used to suggest or claim merely that a given person is *at present happy*; but one might also use it to assert that someone is happy *with the way things are at present*.)

Certain natural reactions to or interpretations of the example we have been focusing on make it important to make some of the distinctions we have been focusing on in the last few pages. But in other examples of failure to comply with rational restrictions on optimizing misunderstanding is perhaps not so likely to occur, and the intuitive plausibility of (some) such restrictions is easier to grasp.

Consider the child who keeps eating more and more cookies long past the point where most of us would be satisfied and would stop. We of course know—what the child may not—that eating so many cookies is likely to have bad effects: spoil one's dinner, give one a stomach ache, add undesirable body weight, and so forth. But whereas such ignorance on the part of a child is understandable, there is another, more problematic aspect to what the child is doing. Even apart from the ill effects of gorging oneself on cookies, the actions and presumed desires of the child strike us as odd. At some point (and apart from the question of ill effects and possible, though hardly inevitable, opportunity costs), the child, we feel, should be content with what she has already eaten, with her previous enjoyment. At some point enough (enjoyment) is enough, and it is high time to stop gorging cookies; and the child's insatiability seems practically irrational for the way it fails to remain within more or less definite limits. (The objection here is clearly neither moral nor consequentialistic.) But when we in this way suppose that the child lacks any sense of when to stop, we do not have to be assuming that the child eventually reaches a point where she is no longer enjoying herself and so is expending effort in vain: if asked, the child might well say that she is continuing to eat the cookies because they taste so good (it is irrelevant that earlier cookies may have been relished *more* than later ones).

On the other hand, neither is it plausible to suppose that the insatiable child suffers some more or less painful or unpleasant longing for cookies which somehow mars or detracts from the pleasures of eating and which somehow therefore ruins the example as an example of irrational optimizing. All along the child may seem and be quite happy occupied as she is. Her problem, as we see it, is having no sense of when enough is enough. So we here have another, and perhaps a more clear-cut or easily recognized example of our common-sense restrictions on individualistic optimizing.

But these common-sense rational restrictions can also be viewed as limitations on the maximization of (expectable) preference-satisfaction. Where such maximization involves the pursuit of personal good beyond what is entirely satisfactory, it is inconsistent with our intuitive notions of individualistic rationality. So the insatiable cookie-eating and house-hunting examples can be used to show the divergence between common-sense practical rationality and the standard inherent in the preference-maximizing view.

However, common-sense *deontological* restrictions, for all their initial intuitiveness and plausibility, have been shown in recent years to have rather problematic, and even unintuitive, implications. And something very similar turns out to be the case with our ordinary rational restrictions. Such restrictions have something quite odd about them that is perhaps best conveyed by considering how someone convinced of the rationality of *optimizing* might respond to the idea of rational restrictions.

II

The defender of an optimizing view of practical rationality might be willing to grant that we commonly assume or presuppose the existence of rational restrictions on optimizing and preference-maximization, but question the validity of such thought or practice. "Look," she might say, "by optimizing beyond the point where everything is perfectly satisfactory or when I have had enough, I am still—as the common-sense view seems only too willing to grant—making things better for myself. How can it be against reason, individualistically irrational, to make certain efforts and do certain things when they knowably lead to one's being better off? Even if, as you argued earlier, it is not rationally incumbent on me to seek or do these things, how can it be rationally incumbent on me *not* to do them, if I know they will improve (or not disimprove) things for me, if I actually *gain* from such action?"

Such remarks do show us, I think, the perspective from which someone who connects rational choice with personal good may wish to criticize common-sense rational restrictions on optimizing; but it is important to notice that this perspective involves an exclusive emphasis on the (knowable) results or consequences for the individual of optimizing beyond the entirely satisfactory. If we limit ourselves to the consideration of the results of such optimizing, then, as the above remarks make clear, our common-sense restrictions do seem very odd, and not very plausible. However, a defender of the restrictions might reply that an exclusive focus on results precisely neglects the considerations that most strongly, and intuitively, favor the existence of rational restrictions on optimizing. We are considering the optimizer who leaves a completely satisfactory situation in order to improve things for himself, and if we focus on the intrinsic character of the situation being left and of the attempt to leave such a situation, rather than (merely) on the results of the successful effort to leave, it is much easier to see the appeal of the idea of common-sense restrictions. What makes transgression of the restrictions seem irrational is the very fact that someone is making an effort to do better for herself in a situation where things are (in the respects relevant to her efforts) entirely satisfactory. Our common-sense objection thus concerns how the optimizer is deliberately acting in relation to her situation and has nothing to do with what we are assuming to be the successful results of such action.

But the staunch defender of optimizing may object here that any judgment of irrationality based on factors other than (intended) consequences leaves out considerations of the utmost importance and that, as we have seen, once we bear in mind that the transgressor of common-sense rational restrictions is deliberately improving things for himself, it becomes difficult to regard his situational behavior—however intrinsically characterized—as objectionable from the standpoint of individualistic rationality. In this way, the rational restrictions that initially seem so plausible may come to be doubted or denied.

The above is more than reminiscent of the on-going dispute in moral theory between the defenders of deontological restrictions and act-consequentialists. Common-sense intuition finds it morally unacceptable for someone deliberately to kill one person to prevent others from dying, as, say, for a surgeon secretly to kill a healthy individual in order to use his organs to save a number of accident victims from dying. But if we focus on the results of such an action—and assume that the killing really would be kept secret and have no untoward consequences for the behavior of others or for the surgeon herself—it is harder to see what she does as morally objectionable. Isn't it objectively worse, a greater tragedy, if several victims die from an accident that is no fault of theirs than if one person is killed by another? And if it is, how can we condemn the surgeon for deliberately bringing about an overall better course of events? But these questions posed by the act-consequentialist focus on the agent's deliberately bringing about *certain results*, rather than on the *way* she does so, on what she has to *do* in her particular circumstances in order to bring about what may be regarded, from an impersonal standpoint, as better results. And just as rational restrictions may seem less odd or puzzling if we keep in mind what the unbounded optimizer is actually, deliberately doing, so too may it help the cause of deontological restrictions to remember what is intrinsically involved in violating them. Furthermore, and this is perhaps already fairly obvious, the rational and deontological restrictions both seem to hang on (the validity of) some sort of distinction between commission and omission, doing and letting happen. The rational requirements not to optimize forbid us actively to seek what is better, deliberately to make things better, when our situation is appropriately satisfactory, but do not seem to rule out in such a situation simply accepting a good thing or improvement that lands in our lap. And of course it is a familiar fact about the deontological restrictions that they seem to invoke, for cases of the kind mentioned above, a distinction between deliberate, active killing and passive letting die.

Our common-sense moral restrictions seem subject to a further difficulty which appears to raise no problems for rational restrictions on individual optimizing. Relying on intuition, we seem to be forbidden to kill not only in order to prevent accidental or natural deaths, but even to prevent some much larger number of killings by others. But if killing is so objectionable, it seems odd that it should be objectionable for someone to try to minimize the number of such objectionable acts. The common-sense insistence on the moral objection-ability of killing can lead us to question some of the implications of our common-sense deontological restrictions. And this self-generated problem of our ordinary moral views represents a considerable challenge to them.

However, as Scheffler has pointed out, it is possible to accept deontological restrictions without being committed to the common opinion that it is wrong to kill even in order to prevent a greater number of killings.[9] Deontological restrictions exist if there are possible situations where it is morally impermissible to perform some act whose consequences are (impersonally considered) as good as or better than those of any alternative available to the agent. And the view, roughly, that it is wrong to kill except in order to minimize acts of killing entails such restrictions by forbidding us, for example, to kill one person in order to prevent several accidental deaths. But this view also clearly allows for killing to prevent a larger number of killings and so avoids the self-undermining aspect of common-sense morality mentioned above.

For present purposes, furthermore, it is worth noting that our common-sense views on rational choice do not clearly possess the self-undermining character of common-sense deontology. It may be intuitively plausible to hold that it is sometimes irrational to optimize, but nothing in our ordinary view of practical rationality clearly corresponds to the moral notion that it is wrong to prevent killings by killing. In fact, it is very difficult to figure out what the rational analogue of this notion would be. However, given the familiar parallelism between interpersonal moral choice and intertemporal, but intrapersonal rational choice, the closest analogue would seem to be something like: it is irrational to optimize beyond what is entirely satisfactory at a given time even as a means of preventing a larger number of such acts in the future. And this idea lacks the forceful intuitive applicability of its moral analogue.

Thus consider (the example is from Shelly Kagan) a reformed compulsive optimizer who has his former habits under control except for occasional lapses. Having thus achieved a satisfactory level of non-compulsion, would it be irrational, compulsive, of him to seek to wipe out all his (future) lapses and achieve perfect non-compulsion? If so, then there is a common-sense rational analogue of the moral requirement not to violate deontological restrictions in order to prevent other violations. However, what is satisfactory need not be entirely satisfactory, and it is far from clear, even in common-sense terms, that things are entirely—or in every way—satisfactory when one still has some tendency toward compulsive behavior. (Our discussion of the pursuit of ideals, later in the present chapter, will serve to reinforce this point.) So I think that the attempt to achieve complete non-compulsion may not violate any common-sense rational restriction on optimizing, and it may in fact be impossible to devise an example where things are entirely satisfactory and where it seems irrational to optimize beyond that point in order to prevent one's own future violations of a restriction on optimizing. In that case our common-sense moral restrictions may have a questionable aspect for which there is no precise parallel in common-sense views of practical rationality, and the latter may therefore actually have the better credentials. But we have also seen that it is possible to qualify common-sense morality into a view that preserves deontological restrictions, but eliminates its self-undermining tendency. And such a view is perhaps more in line with our most intuitive ideas about rational choice and action.

III

Our description above of putative rational restrictions on individual optimizing should in one sense be entirely familiar: once examples and arguments have been provided, it is not difficult to see that they capture an important aspect of our intuitive thinking and implicit practice in the area of rational choice. But in another sense our account of these matters is not familiar. The idea that, in parallel with common-sense deontological restrictions, there may be rational restrictions applicable to the individualistic pursuit of the good, lacks clearcut philosophical antecedents.

That is not to deny that there have been previous advocates of moderation or of limits or restrictions on the individual's pursuit of her own good. As I have already mentioned in previous chapters, the Epicureans do advocate such limitations; but the limitations are justified, fundamentally, in instrumental terms. We are to avoid unnecessary or intense pleasures because doing so is a (likely) means to a greater overall balance of pleasure/happiness over pain/unhappiness, and is, more particularly, the only way we are likely to approximate to an existence free of pain and suffering.

However, as may already be apparent and will in any case be made clearer in what follows, such instrumental justification is not what lies behind the intuitions unearthed in our earlier discussion of common-sense rational restrictions. Even without considering possible effects of optimizing, something seems to be inherently irrational about trying to do better when things are already satisfactory in every way, and indeed the mainstay of our explication of this intuition—the idea that things can be in every way satisfactory without being as good as possible—appears basically unrelated to any argument from means and ends.

But that does not yet invalidate an instrumental argument,

roughly following the Epicurean line of thought, in support of rational restrictions on optimizing. If the general tendency to optimize results in less good for the individual over the long run, then a habit of satisficing in certain sorts of situations may have much to recommend it and the justification of such a habit or tendency is then naturally thought to show that rational restrictions on optimizing can be established on an instrumentalist foundation. Richard Sylvan, Philip Pettit, and a number of other philosophers and economists have recently been suggesting arguments of this kind based on a wide variety of instrumentalist considerations. But considerable difficulties attach to this line of thought, and we must bring these to light in order to recognize the gulf that separates such instrumentalist conceptions of satisficing and rational restrictions from our ordinary thinking about these matters.

The view I have labeled instrumentalist is based on the idea that the habit of satisficing may well have optimal long-run consequences for the individual and so too the general tendency to rest content with what is entirely satisfactory though less than the best achievable through action. The habit or tendency may then be said to be rational or rationally acceptable, and habits or tendencies of choice with less good results for the individual may then be held rationally unacceptable. But all this represents as yet a form of instrumentalism (or person-relative consequentialism) applicable only to the rational assessment of habits or tendencies of practical thought and action. Nothing has yet been said about the rationality or irrationality of particular choices, and since rational restrictions on optimizing are primarily conceived as applying to particular choices or actions, we must add to the views sketched above in order to have any sort of instrumentalist account or justification of those restrictions.

It should be clear, however, what the next step would naturally be. The instrumentalist can say that a particular choice is rational or rationally acceptable if it is in accordance with a rationally acceptable practical tendency or habit: particular acts are to be justified in terms of the general tendencies or dispositions they exemplify, and the irrationality of optimizing on a given occasion when things are entirely satisfactory will derive from the less-than-optimal character of the results, for the individual, of the general tendency to optimize (in such circumstances). Now I have described this form of instrumentalist justification in very general terms, because different philosophers have put the argument in differing ways and because I believe the problems with this approach are quite independent of the details of given formulations. Instrumentalism about rational restrictions or permissions is rather closely parallel to the Rule-Utilitarian or Rule-Consequentialist justification of deontological restrictions and permissions, and as such it suffers from many of the same problems.

Again roughly speaking, Rule-Consequentialism and Rule-Utilitarianism judge the validity of moral rules in terms of the consequences for everyone of having (or accepting or following) such rules, and they judge the morality of actions in terms of whether they fall under valid rules, thereby making the moral acceptability of an act into a function of the consequences of the rule (or set of rules) it exemplifies, rather than of the consequences of the act itself. In recent years this position has been criticized for being imperfectly or inconsistently consequentialist. Defenders of utilitarianism and anti-utilitarians alike have become increasingly dissatisfied with the way Rule-Utilitarianism applies the test of consequences to rules but not to individual acts. No justification for this difference has found any sort of wide acceptance, and indeed if we are willing to apply the test of optimal consequences, the dictates of impersonal all-knowing benevolence, to rules and sets of rules, it seems inconsistent, when we know a given act would have best consequences and would be preferred from the ideal standpoint of rational benevolence, to label that act morally unacceptable because it contravenes rules whose general acceptance is morally preferable or required. Why should the favorable evaluation of general rule automatically yield a favorable evaluation of some particular act which, though it falls under that rule, fails to serve the very ends which justify the rule in the first place?

Nor can the Rule-Utilitarian or Rule-Consequentialist reply that a given failure to comply with a useful rule will likely undermine the rule's usefulness and so be ruled out for reasons of that sort: the effects on compliance with or respect for the rule are already included in the reckoning that tells us that on this particular occasion failure to comply will have overall better effects than complying. And so where it is clear that compliance would have worse effects, it seems a form of rule-worship inconsistent with the spirit of consequentialism and with the justification that has already been given for having (generally complying with) certain general rules to insist that one should follow the rule in the given instance nonetheless.

Such indirect consequentialism (evaluating acts in terms of the consequences of some other entity) has fallen into disrepute—at least into disrepair—in recent years,[10] and recent proponents of the idea of evaluating particular choices derivatively from our assessment of the rationality of certain general habits of choice have failed to realize that their view is open to the same charge of inconsistency that is so widely agreed to fit Rule-Utilitarianism. These philosophers urge us to judge the rational acceptability of habits of decision-making or choice according to their optimific character. Yet they tell us to judge the rationality of particular decisions or choices indirectly, in terms not of their own consequences, but of the consequences of something else: the habits and tendencies they exemplify. However, on a given occasion a particular choice may have knowably better consequences for the agent than the choice that exemplifies the general tendency with best consequences for the agent. How can it then be irrational to "go against" the optimal general tendency if the tendency itself is justified in terms of its optimal consequences?

Proponents of indirect instrumentalism about rationality offer us no reason why we shouldn't, in all consistency, apply the direct test of optimal consequences for the agent equally to habits and to particular choices. And of course if we do, then on those occasions when the choice with best individual consequences fails to exemplify the habit that in general most favors the individual, that choice will nonetheless count as rational (and alternative choices irrational), and we will therefore lack any way to show the irrationality of optimizing when things are already satisfactory in every way. The instrumental method of justifying rational restrictions on optimizing and the acceptability of satisficing seems inconsistent and implausible in much the same way Rule-Consequentialism does. (Later, we shall also be questioning the instrumentalists' assumption that we must evaluate the rationality of habits in terms of whether their consequences are *optimal* for agents.)

The instrumentalist conception of rational restrictions is not, in any event, the way we ordinarily view such restrictions. In parallel with what has been said about the common-sense view of satisficing choices, we do not ordinarily regard the attempt to go beyond the entirely satisfactory as irrational solely because of the long-run ill effects of making such efforts. We may believe that those who always eke out the most and best from situations are more likely to be unhappy when things are not going well and opportunities for improvement scarce. But what seems irrational about insatiable pursuit of one's own good, of good things, is not, fundamentally, a matter of indirect consequences. Intuitively, something is inherently irrational about certain kinds of optimizing, just as, for moral common-sense, something is inherently wrong with the infringement of deontological restrictions. To be sure, the common-sense view of deontological restrictions is open to question and faces a number of very serious problems; nonetheless, at the present time Act-Consequentialism seems to regard common-sense morality as a much more interesting target of criticism than Rule-Consequentialism. And by the same token, I think we may now leave the instrumental view of rationality behind and focus our attention on the conflict between optimizing/maximizing views and the ordinary view of rational choice. To the extent that so much current moral theory centers on the dispute between common-sense morality and act-consequentialism, it behooves us to see whether a similar conflict exists between the ordinary and optimizing/maximizing views of practical rationality, and if so, whether that fact may not have important bearing on the parallel dispute in moral theory.

But having seen that instrumentalism about extramoral rationality, an idea whose roots go back to classical antiquity, yields a view of rational restrictions very different from that of common-sense rationality, we must still ask whether any other philosophical conception of rational choice comes closer to our ordinary view of the restrictions. Has any philosopher or economist ever said that there can be something *inherently* irrational about certain kinds of optimizing?

IV

I believe Aristotle comes as close as anyone to explicitly accepting inherent limitations on rational optimizing. But rather than attempt to give a scholarly account of aspects of his work that might be relevant to this assessment, let me just mention some highlights about which there seems to be fairly widespread agreement. For Aristotle, a right or rational action (he does not clearly distinguish them) lies in a mean between extremes, and an unjust or intemperate action fails to be medial. Virtue, of course, requires more than the doing of acts prescribed by virtue, the doing of appropriately right or rational acts, but Aristotle is nonetheless sometimes accused of having an instrumental view of the (moral) virtues, of treating acts in accordance with them merely as means to a good life for particular individuals and as having, from the internal standpoint of the virtuous person, a merely contingent force and validity based on their perceived connection to his happiness. Certainly a good deal of the Aristotelian text can be, or at any rate has been, interpreted in this manner, but the evidence is striking in favor of a quite different view according to which Aristotle regards virtue and various virtuous acts as having to a very large extent an inherent, non-instrumental, validity or rightness. Aristotle shows an appreciation of the intrinsic appeal of non-egoistic moral considerations, and his views about the dictates of practical reason are thus not as instrumentalist as what we find in Epicureanism.[11]

However, we are seeking historical antecedents for the idea of non-instrumental, extramoral rational restrictions on optimizing, and Aristotle's emphasis on inherent moral considerations, while it erodes the charge of instrumentalism, makes it in fact very dubious whether he is a defender of rational restrictions in the sense intended here. For remember that the limits on optimizing that we have described as being part of the common-sense view of individualistic rationality were in no way moral requirements; we have argued that quite apart from what one may or may not want to say in moral criticism of the unlimited pursuit of good things, such behavior is simply irrational. But Aristotle does tend to run together moral and rational requirements, and in particular passages where he comes closest to defending intrinsic limitations on individual optimizing, his argument is so fraught with moralism as to make it doubtful that what he has in mind are purely egoistic or self-regarding extramoral rational restrictions. Let me give you some examples.

Aristotle's discussion of *pleonexia*, of graspingness, describes the grasping individual as wishing and striving for more than his fair share of goods.[12] He is contrasted with the just individual who sees what is right and rational for himself to want when goods are being apportioned, and who wants no more and no less than he deserves. The *pleonektes* thus counts

as irrational, but also unjust and blameworthy. So graspingness is as much a moral as a rational fault for Aristotle, and it is
perhaps not inaccurate to say that he treats it as a rational fault
because he regards it as a moral fault. Aristotle's discussion
nowhere suggests that pleonexia may involve an over-
reachingness, a greediness that is inappropriate or irrational
quite apart from its predictable effect on the interests of others.

Yet the term "pleonexia" can be translated as "greediness,"
and as we saw earlier, the child who takes more and more and
more cookies is naturally considered irrational for being
greedy in this way quite independently of anyone else's being
deprived of a fair share. Indeed, someone who could curb
herself when the interests of others were at stake, but who
would otherwise tend to eat cookies endlessly, still seems
irrationally compulsive to us. So by focusing on the negative
moral aspects of pleonexia, Aristotle misses out on those
aspects that are rationally criticizable quite apart from the
suggestion of moral fault (and apart from their bad consequences for the agent). Aristotle may approach, but he here
fails to home in on, the extramoral rational restrictions that
ordinary thinking implicitly assumes for individual optimizing. Greediness can be a moral fault, and it can be irrational for
instrumentalist reasons, but it can also be regarded as irrational
for inherent, non-moral reasons.

However, Aristotle discusses immoderation in other places.
In the course of describing household management and the
acquisition of private property in Book I of the *Politics*, he
contrasts two modes of wealth-getting: natural and unnatural.
The first is a part of the art of household management, involves barter but not money, and has as its limited aim the
satisfaction of the needs of the members of a household. The
other, which enters into retail trade and other uses of money,
seeks riches and property without inherent limit; it involves
going beyond life's necessities, beyond what is enough, and it
has no proper role to play in the good life.

Here we clearly have some sort of anticipation not only of the idea that it can be rational to seek no more than one needs, but also of the idea that it is irrational to have a limitless or insatiable desire for wealth. But Aristotle states these views in such a way that, once again, it is impossible to disentangle rational considerations from moral ones. He says, for example, that household management for the sake of life's necessities is both natural and honorable, but that the acquisition of money and unneeded property is unnatural and justly censured. (Usury is described as the most unnatural and most hated way for men to gain wealth.)

In marked contrast, then, with the frequent accusation that Aristotle subordinates the moral to the individual pursuit of happiness, it would seem that the Aristotelian critique of insatiability, unlimited acquisitiveness, and the like is overly moralized.[13] Even if there is something morally objectionable about these things, a common-sense rational criticism of them can be made quite apart from any moral considerations, but this is a fact Aristotle fails to recognize (one wonders here about relevant differences between Greek and modern society).

Of course moral, or moralistic, criticism of immoderation and unlimited desire is rife not only in Aristotle, but in the everyday thinking of many people today. Moral and rational criticism of excess or insatiability are commonly entangled, and little attempt has been made to distinguish them. Clearly, instrumentalist rational criticisms of immoderation and the like are frequently lumped together with moral objections, and it takes careful analysis to separate those factors (and assign to each its proper critical weight). And by the same token, it takes the careful sifting of examples in order to disentangle the intrinsic rational considerations described in this chapter from both the moral and the instrumental rational criticisms that can be directed at insatiability and immoderation. Thus as we saw earlier, our surprise and perplexity at the gluttony or greediness of the insatiable cookie-eater is not founded on instrumentalist considerations, nor yet on moral considerations concerning likely unjust actions. And they are certainly not usually based on moral-religious views about the sin of gluttony. The things we have to say against insatiable cookie-eating follow a well-trodden path between the purely rational instrumentalist critique of the Epicureans and the non-instrumental moralism invoked by Aristotle or the Church, bringing together elements from each and discarding elements from both. For common-sense rational restrictions on optimizing are neither moral nor instrumentalist, but are instead grounded in intrinsic and purely rational practical considerations.

V

In the foregoing discussion I have been deliberately vague about two significant issues: I have not said how close to optimality the entirely satisfactory lies and so have not given the rational restrictions of common sense a precise location on what we might call the "vertical axis." But a number of "horizontal" issues have also been left vague or fudged: even if satisficing is rationally *permissible* in every area of human good, we still need to consider whether rational *restrictions* on optimizing apply across the entire range of human choice and actions. (The further question of whether and how the vertical varies with the horizontal is for present purposes perhaps best left alone.)

The scope of the rational restrictions is vague because of vagueness about what counts as satisfactory. We have assumed that ordinary thinking can be rationally tolerant of moderate choices and of choices that aim for better than what moderation would require; we have assumed that at the one end asceticism, and at the other insatiability, are commonsensically irrational. But that still doesn't tell us how far short of the obtainable or hoped for optimal the rational restrictions take hold.[14] Perhaps one can frame rough-and-ready general guides to what is or is not entirely satisfactory; perhaps such matters are best (or inevitably) left to intuitive judgment. It is hard to be sure either way, but it does seem clear that the situation here is not remarkably different from what we encounter on many important issues of common-sense morality.

Consider, for example, the deontological restrictions common morality is said to impose on impersonal optimizing. It is supposed to be morally unacceptable to kill one person in order to save a number of others, but even those who accept such a restriction typically refuse to accept it in a fully generalized form. They hesitate to say that it must be wrong to kill one innocent person to prevent a catastrophic (or great) loss of life. Making a number of simplifying assumptions, we may feel it is wrong to kill one to save five, but be fairly sure it would not be wrong to kill one to save millions; and it may not be very clear to us what to say about killing one person to save twenty others. Our intuitive sense of right and wrong does not speak univocally and really seems to fail us in such questions of numbers, so it would seem that common-sense morality accommodates a certain degree of vagueness within its deontological restrictions. It may insist that for *some* number greater than one, and given various simplifying assumptions, it is wrong to kill one person to save that number of (other) people, but remain vague about the specification, even the rough specification, of the number.[15] The common-sense restrictions on individual optimizing possess a similar vagueness: it is supposed to be irrational to try to surpass *some* entirely satisfactory level of personal good short of the optimal; but we are apparently given no specific dictates—none at any rate come immediately to mind—about the (vertical) location of the entirely satisfactory.

Let me, finally, say something about the various respects or areas in which it can be irrational, sometimes, to optimize. Until now we have mainly focused on material and sensual well-being, using examples involving eating and housing. The question thus quite naturally arises whether the restrictions have intuitive application across all the different areas of personal good, or whether our previously chosen examples indicate that the restrictions are limited to "lower" pleasures and material goods or satisfactions.

I think it can be made clear that the restrictions are not limited to the material and the purely sensual. Common-sense rational limits, for example, seem to characterize our desires for intimacy and affection. Consider the ordinary notion of uxoriousness, which involves either subservience to one's wife or (more relevantly for present purposes) being excessively affectionate toward, doting on, one's wife. Our common notion of excess here is independent of any idea of injustice or wrongdoing or of the unfortunate results of doting on a spouse. A person constantly affectionate with his wife, a person so eager for such exchange of affection that he is reluctant to go off on business trips or even to go to work seems ridiculous quite apart from any consequences of such behavior. Even if the marriage is strengthened—the wife dotes on him—and he always tears himself away when business would really suffer if he stayed, his doting seems irrational.[16] Surely, at some point the man (rationally) ought to stop feeling the need for more exchanges of affection. It is not that we think that such continuing affection is not a good or enjoyable thing for him, but rather that in this area, as with gustatory pleasures, at some point enough is enough. To be sure, we think his behavior and transparent desires unseemly and weak, and these notions blend with the moral; but any such quasi-moral repugnance will almost certainly also combine with a sense that his greediness, his insatiable desire, for affection is as childishly and compulsively irrational as an insatiable desire to eat cookies—comparisons of this sort are indeed likely to occur to us when we seek for ways of saying why we find it difficult, or impossible, to make rational sense of the excessively affectionate husband.

Here is another example in this general area. Consider someone known to have many intimate and good friends who one day announces that he wants to get involved in such-and-such activity or travel to such-and-such place in the hope of making new friends. We remind him, let us imagine, that he already has many very good friends, and his response is that friendship is a wonderful thing—as he already so thoroughly knows—and that that is precisely his reason for wanting to have additional intimate friends. "If I'm so lucky," he says, "to have the friends I do, think how much better off I'd be with even more friends."

Now this retort seems both specious and bizarre; it is hard to make human sense of it. But is that because we doubt that the person in question will be better off for having put himself in a position to form additional friendships; do we think the possible new friendships are not worth the effort? Doesn't the real oddness here lie in the person's desire for a larger number of intimate relationships when with respect to the good of friendship things already seem so thoroughly satisfactory for him? Of course, a possible additional complication is that his remarks make us doubt his very capacity for genuine intimacy, or real friendship; his seemingly irrational need for more than he has may strike us as a betrayal of intimacy, an untrueness to friendship and to particular friends. But even then we need not suppose that he doesn't stand to gain from his new efforts: it will just be unclear what he expects, or is likely to gain from them. And so in addition to any other problems he may have, the person we have imagined seems irrational for failing to be satisfied with what ought to satisfy anyone, for failing to recognize in the relevant area when enough is enough.

Our two examples thus show that rational constraints on individual optimizing are not limited to material and sensual goods. Do they perhaps then apply in every area of personal good? Even, for example, to ideals of achievement? We may be encouraged in this direction by some of the things we said about moderation in Chapter 1, where we were able to make sense of the desire simply to be a really fine lawyer like one's mother. And if such a desire is not irrational, perhaps, as we have found in other areas, there are rational limits to what one should desire in the way of personal achievement.

But we must be very careful here. Our sense of the irrationality of insatiable cookie-eating and doting uxoriousness arises at least partly from the childish character of such behavior, whereas the unlimited pursuit of certain ideals of achievement may not strike us, or at least may not so immediately strike us, as similarly childish. It is a commonplace of psychology that unbounded, undisciplined childhood desires are, in the process of maturation, sublimated into or replaced by more adult forms of desire and, in particular, by personally fulfilling ideals that can command our respect and do not seem childish. And perhaps certain ideals, then, can rationally be pursued in a maximizing or optimizing manner. Perhaps there is nothing irrational in wanting to be the best lawyer it is possible (for one) to be—where this may even involve being better than (all) other lawyers—because such an unlimited desire is not obviously childish and represents a genuine ideal of achievement at the same time that it aims for a personal good.

But once again we must be careful, because we may encounter limits on rational optimizing whose validity has nothing to do with the contrast between the childish and the adult. The person seeking better and better houses may be irrationally insatiable, but there doesn't appear to be anything particularly childish about that insatiability. The uxorious husband seems childish for depending, hanging, on his wife in the way a child might on a mother. The cookie-eater presumably gobbles the cookies in an overeager, uncontrolled childlike manner. But the pursuer of better and better houses need not be in a hurry or dependent on anyone, so if, as we said, he appears to be irrational, then there can be rational restrictions having to do with something other than apparent childishness.

But even granting all this, the pursuit of professional, scientific, or artistic ideals even when carried on without limit seems somehow different from the house-buying, cookie-eating, and other cases we have been focusing on. The former cases do not give us the immediate sense of irrationality we tend to derive from all the latter. The reason may have something to do with the fact that what is involved are genuine *ideals*. In certain areas of achievement (or personal virtue) we can talk of seeking or attaining not only the best or most, but also the highest. It would not naturally occur to us to think of the house-pursuer as aiming for what is higher (except in price); unless we can tell a long story such a person is not seen as pursuing an ideal, and there is no greatness aimed at in his pursuit of the best (most perfect) possible house. By contrast, the person who seeks to be the best lawyer she can possibly be is naturally thought to be aiming (if only indirectly) at a form of greatness or higher and higher goals/achievements.

A difference between ideal and non-ideal pursuits yields a difference in how we characterize unlimited desire: we would not so readily use the term "compulsive" of someone seeking to be the finest possible lawyer or artist as we would of the relentless pursuer of houses, cookies, or wifely affection. And this may well indicate a deep common-sense reluctance to apply the rational restrictions to the pursuit of genuine ideals. We are reluctant to characterize the latter as compulsive because compulsiveness is regarded as a form of irrationality. The same point emerges from another direction when we consider how much less obvious it seems, in the area of ideals, that things can be entirely, in every way, satisfactory short of the best that might be envisaged or hoped for. It seems much less unreasonable for the artist to feel that things cannot be entirely satisfactory if higher levels remain for him to attain, than for the house-buyer or cookie-eater to have parallel attitudes. (Compare Goethe's remark in the *Italienische Reise*: "In der Kunst ist das Beste gut genug"—"In art the best is good enough.")[17]

However, even if the restrictions fail to apply in areas of ideal personal achievement, some vagueness may well linger in our common-sense notions about the breadth of the restrictions because of unclarity about what exactly counts as a genuine or valid personal ideal. Some people pursue power in an unlimited fashion, and although some of us are inclined to think them irrational, it is certainly possible to speak of an ideal of empire and treat the accumulation of power as a way of achieving greatness. Likewise, given the connection between power and money, even the direct pursuit of wealth may be conceived, by some, as a quest for a kind of greatness, and thus as exemplifying something higher and ideal while at the same time answering to material/sensual needs. (How much more Hegelian than Aristotelian this sounds.) I don't feel in a position to ascribe a view to common sense in this area, and so we are left with horizontal as well as vertical vagueness in our attempt to specify the rational restrictions that are intuitively imposed on individualistic optimizing. We have in any event had a number of quite definite things to say about where the restrictions do apply and where they do not, and we shall have to be content for the moment to leave a number of interesting, but in large measure ancillary, questions unanswered.

Heretofore we uncovered some intuitive grounds for holding that optimization of the individual's own good is not a necessary condition of individualistically rational choice; but rational restrictions on optimizing entail that optimization is insufficient for rational choice and action. Common-sense morality in parallel fashion treats optimization—*impersonal* optimization—as neither necessary nor sufficient for right action. But the analogies between ordinary thinking and ordinary views of rational choice are not limited to those we have been considering, and in Chapter 4 we shall discuss a different sort of common-sense restriction on rational individualistic optimizing that parallels the obligations common-sense morality imposes in virtue of past actions and associations.

· 4 ·

Rational Restrictions Based on Past History

We have just been exploring a major divergence between our intuitive views concerning practical rationality and the optimizing conception that is regarded by many philosophers as the only plausible theory of extramoral rational choice and that is often, in consequence, assumed to be implicit in common-sense practical thinking as well. But the existence of common-sense rational analogues of certain kinds of moral deontology does not, of course, prove that there is an overall common-sense view of rational choice that diverges from the optimizing theory in the many complex ways in which ordinary morality differs from (optimizing) act-consequentialism. Such a larger parallelism does, however, exist, and in the chapters that immediately follow, I hope to elicit this further complexity by relying on the right examples and a number of theoretical considerations. My aim is to show that common-sense ideas, our deep-seated intuitions, about extramoral practical rationality diverge from the optimizing view in most, if not all, of the main ways in which common-sense morality diverges from standard moral consequentialism.

In the present chapter I shall explore some restrictions on rational optimizing whose character is somewhat different from the ones we have already examined, but which have significant analogues within common-sense morality. Later, we shall further develop the overall analogy with a discussion of rational dilemmas, rational supererogation, and rational permissions not to optimize. Although the main emphasis will be on how the common-sense view diverges from the optimizing conception of rational choice, we shall continue to point out the ways in which the former also differs from the preference-maximizing approach to rationality. Both contrasts are essential to a proper understanding of the nature and merits of common-sense rationality, even if the larger interests of ethical theory dictate a primary focus on its relation to the optimizing view.

I

I have been speaking in the plural about the rational restrictions on optimizing explored in the last chapter, but some readers may wish to say that only one such restriction was mentioned: the restriction on trying to make things better for oneself when they are already thoroughly satisfactory. But this last compact formula in fact covers a multitude of rational sins occurring in different areas of the pursuit of human good. According to ordinary thinking, one may be irrationally dissatisfied with one's present level of enjoyment, one's achievements, one's material possessions, or the number of one's personal relationships, and important differences among these (and other) forms of dissatisfaction reflect an underlying many-sidedness to what I have been describing in the plural. By the same token, however, what are usually regarded as a multiplicity of common-sense deontological restrictions can just as easily be encapsulated in a single summarizing formula. The moral requirement not to kill even to achieve better consequences and similar requirements or restrictions in relation to lying, maiming, deceiving, stealing, and torturing can all be seen as instances of a more general moral restriction on treating people badly in the name of overall optimality. But of course this simple formula plays down some important differences, and the same can be said of any single general statement about what it is irrational to do when things are entirely satisfactory.

Now, the above simple formula for deontological restrictions covers impermissible harmings, but also acts, such as lying or deception, which intuitively involve treating someone badly but may not actually cause any harm or suffering to the person treated badly. But all these instances of the formula have a common feature: they are all impermissible doings requiring a minimum of stage-setting. One can harm or lie to someone without having had to do anything oneself in preparation for one's forbidden action. But other deontologically forbidden actions are based in previous history. One can lie to someone one has never met before, but one cannot *break* a promise to someone with whom one has *never* had any previous dealings. One can maim or rape a person on a first encounter, but one cannot let down a friend or relative unless some previous history makes it appropriate to speak in this way. According to common-sense views, it can be wrong not to give preferential treatment to a friend or member of one's family even if one can accomplish more good by doing otherwise. I have an obligation to save my drowning wife, even if I could do more good by rescuing some public figure instead; and if I do not save her, I let her down (and worse); but the wrongness arises from previous circumstances of association and intimacy and cannot, so to speak, be read off from the present situation in which I either save or do not save her.

The distinction between deontological failures that can and those that cannot be conceived apart from past history is not unfamiliar.[1] I have mentioned it because I believe common-sense rational restrictions are subject to a similar duality. To the extent that the thoroughly satisfactory character of a given situation has no essential reference to past history, the rational restrictions of the previous chapter are analogous with moral restrictions on lying and harming. But as we are now about to see, the applicability of various other rational restrictions is clearly based in previous doings and they are therefore analogous to deontological restrictions on breaking promises and letting down one's intimates. The examples to be mentioned will seem familiar and intuitive, but, once again, they have played almost no role in recent theoretical discussions of rational choice. Optimizing theories of rationality are usually forward-looking and therefore preclude rational restrictions on optimizing based on what has happened prior to the time when the restrictions apply. But such backward-looking elements of rationality really do have a place in ordinary thought about choice and action. Backward-looking moral restrictions are a staple of moral theoretic discussion, though of course the moral consequentialist wants to urge their irrationality (consider all the talk of "rule worship"). But it has not been recognized that extramoral practical rationality is subject to a similar division of opinion: that there are intuitive restrictions on optimizing, based on past individual history, which the optimizing theorist of individualistic rationality will doubt or oppose. We must now try to locate or identify these history-based rational restrictions, but in order to do so, I think one further point about past-based moral restrictions will be helpful.

It is often said that our obligations to keep particular promises and help particular friends apply in virtue of our own previous doings and have no validity otherwise. The obligation to keep a promise must be based on some act of promising made by the person under that obligation, and it has similarly been argued that if we have any obligation to friends, family, country, or whatever, they must be incurred through our own previous (voluntary) activity. Is the voluntary activity supposed to have, as its intentional object, the action one comes under an obligation to perform? It is not clear. Intuitively, parents are obligated to care for children who would not exist but for their voluntary activity; but of course the voluntary activity can be entirely separate from any intention to procreate or undertake an obligation to care for (particular) children. But even a requirement of some sort of voluntary activity is open to serious question. May I not owe an obligation of gratitude to parents or country for goods received when I was too young to request or even consent to them? I am not sure we are in a position to give a definitive answer to this question, but what seems to hold constant, independently of how we answer it, is the assumption that *some* sort of previous history must form the basis for obligations of gratitude, of care for children, and the like. Our obligations to the state or our parents may require specific acts or tacit consent to benefits, but even if they do not, such obligations, as well as our obligations to help friends and children and to fulfill given promises, depend on what has happened in the past, and this is the most general feature which uncontroversially separates such obligations from those obligations not to harm or lie which form the major other part of common-sense deontology.

Having said as much, I would now like to point out some rational requirements that are based in previous history and that correspond to the past-based deontological requirements we have just been talking about. If there are times when, because of past events, we are morally forbidden to do what is impersonally optimific, so too, by our common lights, are there occasions when as a result of previous history it is rationally impermissible for an agent to do something that will have best or tied-best consequences for him.

II

Certain facts about an agent's past, quite apart from her relation to other people, can give rise to a rational constraint on her optimizing (with respect to her own good) at a given time.

One way this can happen is through the agent's previous long-standing desires, hopes, or wishes. Thus, for example, a man has always wanted to see the Pyramids, ever since he read books about them as a child. Finally, as an adult, he travels to Egypt and has an opportunity to visit them. But it turns out that he can with equal ease visit the Temple of Karnak at Luxor, and he is told that he would enjoy that just as much, perhaps more, because of its enormous artistic excellence. In that event, believing the person who tells him this, he says: "Well, in that case, let's visit the Temple of Karnak."

Why does this seem odd? Presumably because a person who has always wanted to visit the Pyramids suddenly, when given the opportunity to see them, decides to do something else. But why, after all, should that be odd? The other visit, as he may believe, will be just as interesting, and possibly more so. So why not visit the Temple of Karnak?

But, you say, the man will later regret that he didn't visit the Pyramids, if he goes to the Temple instead. However, given the blasé way he throws over his previous desire to visit the Pyramids, there may be no reason to think he will have such regrets. What seems irrational to us about his actions and attitude—assuming he really does end up visiting the Temple of Karnak—is, rather, the very ease with which he weighs anchor from his past interest in, desire to see, the Pyramids. Even if the man won't regret missing out on the Pyramids, we feel he ought in all consistency to have such regrets, just as, in all consistency, he *ought* to have preferred to visit the Pyramids in the first place. And clearly this is not a moral (nor a purely logical) criticism; it is a criticism of his rationality in acting and reacting as he does. The man lacks a kind of personal consistency over time that makes him difficult to understand, to make sense of: what he does in Egypt fails to "fit in" with his earlier life and its aspirations in particular.

I have just said that the man is not immoral for acting as he does, but the irrationality of his behavior can in part be captured by a comparison with a certain kind of common-sense immorality. Breaking promises is ordinarily thought to be the wrongful violation of past commitments, and someone who sincerely promises to do something at a later time and then blithely does something else instead because he thinks the latter will have overall better results makes a mockery of his earlier promise. His later moral attitude and action seem inconsistent with the attitude behind his earlier promise. By the same token, the visitor to Egypt's sudden shift of desire or intention is a kind of travesty of, and is strangely at variance with, his long-standing desire to visit the Pyramids. And I believe previous desires, hopes, or intentions are naturally thought to set rational limits to subsequent individual optimizing in a fashion analogous to the way in which promises, prior commitments, place moral restrictions on subsequent impersonal optimizing. Just as purely consequentialist thinking seems out of place in someone who has made a promise or commitment, so too does an exclusive regard for good consequences for oneself seem humanly, personally, unacceptable in someone with a long-standing strong (and otherwise reasonable) desire. To say, "I'll get just as much from seeing the Temple of Karnak, so I might just as well see it," when one has always wanted to see the Pyramids and never previously heard of the Temple, seems quirkily changeable, volatile, fickle, capricious, and in this context these are terms of rational, not moral, criticism.[2]

The past thus exerts an influence over what is commonsensically rational or moral in any given present, but the prevalent optimizing view of rational choice and utilitarian-consequentialist conceptions of morality leave such considerations out of account. So we have a second area or respect in which, in parallel with common-sense morality, our ordinary thinking sets restrictions on rational optimizing. And though I have above invoked a parallel between a kind of practical rational consistency and deontological restrictions based on past promises, deontological restrictions based on special relationships would have served just as well. To live, for example, on terms of intimacy with someone and then, without reason, to let her down by treating her on a par with strangers also seems to be a form of inconsistency and to be morally objectionable quite apart from considerations of overall optimality. And we can say that such treatment is not in keeping with, and makes a mockery of, one's previous relationship.

Now of course there are times when breaking one's promise (or letting down a family member) is not optimific and where act-consequentialism can agree with common-sense deontology about the wrongness of doing so. But in relation to such cases the common-sense moral motive for keeping one's promise (or not letting down the family member) will not be a desire for the impersonally optimal but a sense of being constrained by one's previous actions or history. And, similarly, when a person who has always wanted to visit the Pyramids does visit them, it may well be true that he would have regretted not visiting them, so that a visit to the Temple of Karnak would not in fact have had best results for him; but in such a case one doesn't visit the Pyramids in order to avoid the regrets and achieve greater overall optimality. One visits them because one has always wanted to, and indeed we cannot make sense of the potential subsequent regret except in terms of a personally accepted independent reason to see what one has always wanted to see. (We cannot make sense of altruistic motivation by supposing, as in the famous story about Lincoln and the pigs, that it is a mere desire to avoid certain pangs of conscience. The pangs couldn't exist but for some independent source of altruistic motivation.) So even if expectable good is as great or slightly greater on the assumption that one visits Karnak, one has a reason to prefer visiting the Pyramids because of one's previous history. And such reasons emerge not only from the standpoint of the person whose past history thus constrains his present rationality, but in the eyes of other people who may learn about the earlier desire. Having suggested a visit to either the Pyramids or Karnak and learned that you have always wanted to see the Pyramids, I may say: "The two places are of equal interest, but if, as you say, you have always wanted to see the Pyramids, then of course you will want to go there." And such a reply, again, seems to accept the sort of independent, past-based reason we have been describing.

However, as was the case with the rational restrictions not based on past history, rational restrictions based on one's past have their paradoxical aspect. Once again the defender of optimizing individual rationality may find it difficult to understand how it can be irrational to visit Karnak when the results of such a choice are no worse (and possibly better) for one than any alternative. Isn't the insistence (other things being fairly equal) on doing what fits in with past desire a kind of causal ancestor worship making as little sense as the rule worship underlying deontology? (Indeed, requirements to keep promises or give preference to intimates are a moral version of causal ancestor worship.) But given what was said in the last chapter, it should be fairly clear that the defender of common-sense rational, or moral, restrictions has something to say by way of reply. She can criticize the exclusive focus on consequences and claim that the past as well can be relevant to rational choice at a given time: which actions fit in better with one's past can be relevant to what it is rational to do.

Of course, the optimizing theorist of rationality or the moral act-consequentialist may at this point seek to commandeer such considerations in behalf of his own theory. If one's life doesn't make good sense or has incongruous parts when one doesn't act on long-standing strong desires, then someone who acts on such desires may, in addition to the other personal goods he promotes, be promoting the second-order or structural good of having a unified, non-incongruous, non-dissociated life. When one takes such good into consideration, the choice of Karnak may be pretty clearly ruled out on optimizing personal grounds. Certainly this is a move the optimizing theorist can make in her own behalf, but I don't think it undercuts—it may even add strength to—the view that common-sense rationality places limits on individualistic optimizing.

Consider a parallel. Consequentialists and others sometimes say that they can approximate the deontology of promise-keeping within a consequentialist or otherwise non-deontological framework by placing an appropriate intrinsic value on the fact that a promise is kept. The breaking of a promise, which involves, as it were, a kind of moral disunity or inconsistency in the personal history of the agent, is an evil that needs to be reckoned among the effects of promise-breaking, and when it is, according to such theorists, (many) acts of promise-breaking that might otherwise seem to have better overall consequences are seen to have less good results than promise-keeping.[3] Without judging the validity or success of various attempts to approximate deontology within some non-deontological (and typically, act-consequentialist) framework, it seems fairly clear that such reductions or approximations are not attempts to capture the actual modes of thought involved in ordinary deontological thinking; rather, those who offer them may have doubts about the validity of deontology in its own terms and are in any case interested in seeing how fully ordinary deontological claims can be represented, or preserved, within a different framework. But this sort of enterprise does presuppose the existence, within ordinary thinking, of a "spirit" of deontology that is not reproduced (though it may to some extent be vindicated) in the reductions. Something similar can be said of any attempt one might make to reduce rational restrictions based on past history to rational optimizing terms.

The wrongness of breaking promises is not intuitively conceived as a failure to bring about the greatest amount of good, but rather as something inherent in a certain kind of action or action-sequence. And it is not clear to me that anyone would ever have conceived of breaking promises as involving some kind of higher-order intrinsic evil, if deontological thinking hadn't been so prevalent. By the same token, attempts to reduce rational restrictions based on past history to individualistic optimizing terms in no way argue against the existence of distinctive rational restrictions governing our ordinary thought and action. Perhaps the man who visits Karnak brings about a higher-order evil of disunity for himself and thereby fails to optimize. But the person who prefers to visit the Pyramids because of his long-standing desire need not do so out of a belief or fear that he will otherwise create less good for himself; certainly he is not likely to be thinking of disunity as an evil he ought to avoid. It makes more sense to suppose instead that he considers the very fact of his long-standing desire as rationally decisive in favor of seeing the Pyramids and against going to Karnak, and as we have seen, this commonplace attitude is also likely to be reflected in his host's views about which place he ought to visit.

A similar response can be made to various other ways in which one might try to show that the man of our example will fail to optimize if he visits Karnak. For example, in *Reasons and Persons* Derek Parfit speculates on the possibility that the fulfillment of one's long-standing desires may be good for one quite apart from whether one has kept the desires and from whether one learns of the fulfillment or experiences anything as a result of the fulfillment,[4] and on such a view the man in the Pyramids case may actually lose out if he doesn't visit them. But, again, I don't think we can account for our tendency to think of the man in the example as irrational in terms of the loss of such a recherché good. If the personal good of having a long-standing desire fulfilled, or of having a more unified life, really were commonsensically relevant to the rationality of the man in the Pyramids example, it would be natural to say: "How imprudent (or short-sighted) of him to go to Karnak, even if that is just as interesting, having always wanted to see the Pyramids!" But such a statement is not at all natural, and that is because the irrationality in the example is not intuitively attributable to any failure to optimize. The man who visits Karnak shows himself to be fickle, capricious, flighty, and as such practically irrational. But clearly it is the man's inconsistency or inconstancy of purpose, not any sense of forgone personal goods, that grounds these attributions of flightiness, caprice, and fickleness; and to the extent the latter notions are inherently critical, common-sense rational criticism of the man who visits Karnak is based on something other than an optimizing standard. In common-sense terms, even if the man loses—or seems to lose—nothing by visiting Karnak, he demonstrates an irrational flightiness, volatility, inconstancy, or what-have-you; and this is tantamount to a rational restriction on optimizing based on considerations of consistency with the past.

But let me say again that I am not defending our ordinary beliefs in these matters. The paradoxical aspects of common-sense moral or rational thinking may make it advisable to reject such thinking or try to salvage its more acceptable elements within a sophisticated consequentialist (or other) framework. But it is important to see that, apart from these issues of validity, our ordinary standards of practical rationality involve rational restrictions on optimizing based on certain facts about the rational chooser's past history—restrictions analogous to those imposed by ordinary deontology in virtue of past commitments, intimacies, and actions. We have found a further way in which ordinary rationality differs from the widespread optimizing model.

III

We may now want to ask whether restrictions based on past history are limited to examples of the precise sort we have discussed or whether they range more widely within ordinary thinking. Our sole previous example was based on a long-standing desire/hope/conditional intention. The flightiness or fickleness in the Pyramids case involved being changeable or inconsistent over time in regard to one's desires or intentions. But one can also be fickle and flighty with respect to one's habits, attitudes, interests, and indeed with respect to a wide range of conative or affective modes. Across this range sudden or frequent changes are normally seen as irrational as well (more particularly) as flighty, inconsistent, capricious, volatile, fickle, or what have you. Individual optimizing, then, is in our ordinary thinking governed by a rational requirement not to be fickle and inconsistent in one's actions and interests; and in a wide variety of cases making a change seems irrational even though it makes the agent no worse off (perhaps even better off) than she otherwise could be.[5] We have discussed one sort of case where a rational restriction on optimizing may apply; here is another.

Imagine someone who is always changing his hobby or avocation. Perhaps he is easily bored and the changes allow him to escape boredom, but another scenario is possible: some new hobby or occupation catches his fancy and distracts or tempts him away from the one he has been avidly pursuing, without there being any question of his having been bored with the latter. And perhaps this often happens with him. In that case, he will seem to us flighty, fickle, capricious, irrationally changeable. But we need not assume he is failing to optimize when we make these judgments. It may well be that he will enjoy the new interest every bit as much as he has been enjoying the old; but he needn't assume that he will enjoy it much more than he would have been able to enjoy the old hobby, if the new one hadn't become available or occurred to him. It is rather that, the new hobby having caught his attention, he is now no longer interested in the old; the new avocation is all he cares about, and so he starts pursuing it.

What seems to us irrational about such shifts of attention,

interest, and activity is their sudden and capricious character. A person who frequently acts this way will, as I have suggested, appear flighty and fickle and inconsistent. Perhaps the man is never disappointed, always enjoys his new pursuits as well as the (for him) exciting changes to yet further interests; but this will seem to most of us a very odd way to live and enjoy life. But the oddness has little if anything to do with morality. Someone fickle with those he loves may be morally objectionable, but I think it is possible to be fickle, or capricious, with respect to certain personal interests without having any tendency to treat people badly or inconsistently, and what we find odd or objectionable about the person who capriciously abandons hobbies for sudden new interests has little to do with his morals and focuses rather on the way he, over time, conceives and pursues his own good, on what seem to be defects or deficiencies of individualistic practical rationality.

One possible line of objection arises at this point. In *A Theory of Justice*, Rawls puts forward an Aristotelian Principle according to which, roughly, people take more pleasure in doing things as they become more proficient at them and prefer more complex and demanding activities to less complex and demanding ones.[6] Doesn't that mean that someone who keeps shifting to new activities will suffer diminutions of enjoyment as she goes from greater proficiency to lesser? But Rawls deliberately refrains from saying that the Principle applies to everyone: he allows that some people might achieve their greatest fulfillment or enjoyment counting blades of grass and rationally plan their lives around that activity. And so it is left open that someone might receive the most pleasure over time from a constantly shifting interest in different activities.

What I want to say is that such an inconstant, flighty life pattern is rationally criticizable apart from issues of total fulfillment or enjoyment, and indeed Rawls, with his persistent emphasis on long-range life-planning, would have some reason to endorse this notion. But I think that even if one doubts (as I do)[7] that long-range life-planning is a requirement of practical rationality, one may believe that something irrational characterizes sudden or capricious shifts of interest and activity and that the frequency and number of such shifts contributes to the picture of an overall irrational life or series of activities. It seems intuitively to be a condition of living intelligently, or sensibly, that one should not shift one's interests, or way of life, at every turn, and this gives us a different sort of example of the way in which one's past has a rational claim on one's future. Earlier interests and occupations may have a rational inertia that can constrain or restrict (the rationality of) subsequent optimization.

Though we have so far been framing the issues in terms of the optimizing model of individualistic rationality, it is not difficult to transpose our discussion of past-based restrictions into relation with the preference-maximizing model of rational choice. To be sure, the man in the Pyramids example is irrational for failing to fulfill a long-standing desire or preference, and so the example might actually be thought to support, or be readily accommodated by, a preference-maximizing scheme. But this thought runs together two senses of "preference-maximization." In failing to fulfill a preference or desire he no longer has, the man in the Pyramids example may fail to maximize the fulfillment of all the different preferences he has over the course of his life, but at the time he chooses Karnak over the Pyramids he may well be acting to maximize the satisfaction of the preferences he has *at that time*, and the pure preference model of rationality is standardly understood as entailing maximization only in this latter sense. In the relevant sense, then, it may well be preference-maximizing to visit Karnak, and the common-sense irrationality of doing so cannot, therefore, be accounted for by appealing to the preference-maximizing model.

Moreover, even a conception of rationality that demands

that one act to maximize the satisfaction of all the different desires or preferences one has over time cannot really handle the various examples we have been discussing. Interest in a given hobby or activity need not involve any long-range plans or desires, and in that case, someone who switches capriciously or flightily from one such activity or hobby to another may satisfy her preferences over time just as fully as she would have if she hadn't made these changes.[8] What is irrational about such changes of activity or interest cannot, therefore, be accounted for in terms of failure of maximization in this sense; and in addition, of course, the flighty individual who shifts from one activity to another may at any given time be maximizing the satisfaction of the preferences she has at that time. So the irrational changeableness or inconsistency of such a person cannot be captured or explained in any kind of preference-maximizing terms;[9] and our common-sense views about such cases thus entail an extramoral rational restriction that forbids one to maximize (expectable) preference-satisfaction in certain fickle, inconsistent, flighty ways.[10]

In conclusion, I would like to call attention to the richness of the vocabulary we have been using both here and in the previous chapter to give expression to common-sense rational criticism. The richness may come as something of a surprise, given our tradition's long-standing commitment to optimizing or maximizing models of rationality, because such models simplify and unify the terms of rational criticism relative to everyday views. Instead of a variety of ways in which one can fail of practical rationality, an optimizing or maximizing view sees only one fundamental way in which action and choice may be irrational. All practical inadequacies connect with a failure to optimize or maximize, and although there is more than one term to describe failure of this kind—"impulsive," "imprudent," "negligent," and so on—the list of such terms is much more limited than what we encounter in letting down the floodgates of perfectly ordinary rational criticism.

In a similar way, the replacement of the many basic sources

of ordinary moral criticism with a single (utilitarian) act-consequentialist standard narrows the essential terms of moral criticisms and leads, from the standpoint of common-sense, to an impoverishment of our moral arsenal. But at least common-sense morality has been recognized as a distinct possibility in ethics, and its richer vocabulary has been seen as available and as a potential weapon for rallying support to common-sense, or more intuitively based, morality. Notions like deceit, dishonesty, injustice, maltreatment, and untrustworthiness, though they have not played a fundamental role in consequentialist theories, have at least been seen for what they are and have been used by moral theorists who felt the need for them. By contrast, the very possibility of a common-sense alternative to the optimizing/maximizing type of rationality has been ignored, and so the distinctive terms of common-sense rational criticism have either been ignored or misconstrued as exclusively tied to moral or instrumentalist rational criticism. But the notions we have been using above—greed, insatiability, volatility, caprice, childishness, fickleness, uxoriousness, flightiness, compulsiveness—are only part of the rich vocabulary available for common-sense (non-instrumental, extramoral) rational criticism, and the possibility of a common-sense alternative to optimizing and maximizing views of individual rationality gives such terms an important new role in ongoing philosophical debate.

· 5 ·

Rational Dilemmas and Rational Supererogation

We have now delved for some time into two major ways in which common-sense practical rationality sets limits on the pursuit of individual good, ways in which, according to ordinary thinking, extramoral individualistic optimizing (and preference-maximizing) can be irrational. The possibility of such rational restrictions may come as something of a surprise, but in that case we may have more surprises in store. It is commonly agreed that there are times when it is rationally impermissible *not* to optimize, but those occasions may be more limited than has been assumed—though they certainly do exist. And it now appears that at least in common-sense terms there can be different ways in which it is rationally impermissible *to* optimize. So more kinds of rational restrictions may be mustered than have been dreamt of in previous philosophy, and that proliferation in turn raises the possibility and prospect of unsuspected forms of *practical rational conflict*.

In recent years literature on the topic of moral dilemmas has been growing. The notion of a moral dilemma—of a situation in which through no prior moral fault of her own, an individual finds it impossible to avoid wrongdoing and objective guilt—is highly controversial; there has been a great deal of discussion about whether common-sense morality and even utilitarianism allow for the possibility of such dilemmas. But

the analogous idea of individualistic rational dilemmas—
where through no practical fault of one's own one finds it
impossible to act rationally—has scarcely been broached. Yet
a consideration of the possibility of rational dilemmas may not
only cast light on the merits of the case for moral dilemmas,
but introduce a topic of considerable independent interest.
And I believe that the case for practical rational dilemmas is as
strong as what can be said in favor of the possibility of moral
dilemmas.

In the present chapter I shall pursue the case for rational
dilemmas and at the same time continue the attempt to demonstrate parallels between common-sense morality and the
common-sense view of rational choice. Our ordinary ideas
about practical rationality are capable of yielding putative
rational dilemmas which parallel some of the best known, and
controversial, examples of common-sense moral dilemma.
But it has also been widely assumed that (utilitarian) act-
consequentialism and the optimizing model of self-regarding
rationality are, respectively, incapable of yielding moral or
rational dilemmas, and I shall be arguing that optimizing
views of morality and rationality (and common-sense to the
extent it too prescribes optimizing) have an unsuspected capacity for producing dilemmas. It will turn out that in order to
avoid rational dilemma, the theory of rational choice will need
to consider the unsettling possibility that, in parallel to what is
frequently said about non-consequentialist morality, there
may be such a thing as rational supererogation, that is, supererogatory degrees of practical rationality. But this last
topic is best left alone until our unfolding discussion of rational
dilemmas forces us to consider it.

I

For there to be a rational dilemma, there must be a situation in
which, through no practical fault of her own, an agent finds it

impossible to act rationally, to make a rational choice among two or more alternatives. To see whether such a thing is possible, let us try to model such a situation on considerations in the area of practical rationality that parallel the factors that are said, by defenders of moral dilemma within common-sense morality, to give rise to moral dilemmas.

In the most frequently discussed putative case of moral dilemma, Agamemnon has to choose between violating his duty as a parent and violating his duty as the leader of a military expedition, and defenders of the view that his situation is truly (morally) tragic have held that each of these duties applies with undiminished force despite the existence and applicability of the other.[1] That is, neither duty overrides the other so as to make it right not to fulfill the other; rather, both have their full force as duties, all things considered, and for that reason Agamemnon must incur guilt (not just an obligation to make amends) whatever he decides to do.

Those who characterize this case as a moral dilemma hold that each of the conflicting obligations or duties has moral force of its own, and that the superiority of common-sense morality over consequentialism lies in the fact that it allows for such varying sources of moral obligation and thus can accommodate the complexity of the moral life. The existence of dilemmas is but one illustration, according to this view, of the richness, subtlety, and difficulty of the moral life. Now whether consequentialism or utilitarianism really is banned from the enjoyment of this intellectual bounty is a question to which we shall return a little later. For the moment let us consider whether any structure similar to what arguably exists in Agamemnon's situation of tragic choice can be found in any case of rational decision-making. Can precepts or principles of practical rationality conflict for a given agent in a given situation in such a way that there is no way for the agent to act rationally, no action which it would be rational for her to choose?

We can see what such a situation would have to be like in order to represent a convincing analogue of Agamemnon-type moral dilemmas. There are precepts like "one ought to give weight to one's future interests" and "one ought not take unnecessary chances with one's own life" which can readily be regarded as commonsensical prima facie principles of rationality. A Rossian-type view of such precepts would treat them as mutually adjustable and balanceable in such a way that whenever they conflict, one or another or some group of them always takes precedence over, overrides, or outweighs those in conflict with it, with the result that there is at least one rational or rationally justified thing for one to do. But one could question this view by claiming, in parallel with what has been said about Agamemnon's tragic situation, that there is no guarantee that amid the welter of conflicting rational principles there will always be a decision, choice, or action which is rationally justified or rational. The cumulative effect of the rational principles in force in a given situation may be to prescribe *a* without qualification and prescribe *b* without qualification, even though they cannot both be performed, thus leaving the aware intelligent agent with the sense that he cannot act in a rational or justified way in the situation he is in.

This, then, is what a defense of rational dilemmas analogous to what has been said of the Agamemnon example would have to look like. But that still leaves us without a plausible example of such a dilemma. And we have to ask ourselves whether we can plausibly give life to the structure of a rational dilemma based on the Agamemnon choice paradigm of a moral dilemma. Can we suggest any plausible or vivid example where, say, two precepts of rationality conflict and where an agent finds it impossible to fulfill the requirements of rationality, to act rationally? And can we do so without relying precisely on the moral examples that are used to support the idea of moral dilemma? For, of course, the idea that moral precepts or requirements are rational requirements, reasons for action, might allow us to turn examples of moral dilemma into examples of rational dilemma.[2] If Agamemnon is wrong whatever he does, then it is natural (in the light of our own belief in the rationality of acting morally) to characterize his plight as one where whatever choice he made would have been unjustified, where nothing could count as a reasonable practical answer.

But when we began by speculating about the possibility of rational dilemmas, we were looking for a form of dilemma arising outside the usual area of morality and having to do with the impossibility of acting rationally, or justifiably. A practical dilemma based in a moral dilemma was not what we had in mind. What would really interest us would be a case where it was impossible for an individual to act rationally with regard to her purely egoistic or self-regarding aims: a case of individualistic rational dilemma. The Agamemnon example is not of this sort.

Foot mentions a non-moral prudential case where "pressing business has given one overriding reason to go to town" but "one nevertheless *ought* to be at home nursing a cold."[3] But it seems appropriate to treat such a case (Foot herself seems to treat it this way) as understandable in fundamentally Rossian terms, as a case where one rational precept or imperative overrides another, and where, therefore, there is at least one thing it is rational for one to do.

In order to have an example of a rational dilemma, we need to describe a situation where, all things considered, every practical solution is fatally flawed and rationally unacceptable. I have been unable to come up with a plausible example of a rational dilemma in this strong sense that possesses anything like the structure of the Agamemnon example, and not just what we find in Rossian examples of moral or other overriding. But it would be a major, though natural, mistake at this point to give up on the idea of common-sense rational dilemma until some rational parallel to the Agamemnon example could be unearthed. For Agamemnon-style dilemmas are not the only kind possible. These involve conflict between two or more *different* principles or precepts—in our particular case the injunction to protect your family clashes with the injunction to do what is necessary, as commander, to ensure the success of your enterprise.

But as Ruth Marcus has pointed out, a conflict of obligations can arise from a single principle, like the obligation to keep promises, when it turns out that through no fault of one's own one cannot keep all the promises one has made; the promises may be of sufficient weight so that guilt is appropriate whichever one one breaks.[4] An even more persuasive example is Sophie's choice between saving her son or saving her daughter from extermination by the Nazis (in order to save one child she must offer the other for extermination, and if she does nothing, both will be taken).[5] Presumably, her general obligation to care for her children is thwarted by her inability to fulfill both her obligation to her son and her obligation to her daughter, so wrongdoing and a conflict of obligations may seem inevitable, but a single moral principle is behind the conflict: particular obligations derived from application of a single principle cannot both be fulfilled.[6] So not every conceivable or putative (common-sense) example of moral dilemma is based on conflicting general principles.

Marcus goes on to argue that although moral dilemmas can be based on a single principle like that enjoining promise-keeping, act-utilitarian and act-consequentialist moral theories advocating a single principle of right or obligatory action cannot yield dilemmas because such theories base the moral characterization of actions solely on their consequences. For a dilemma to occur, according to Marcus, at least one moral principle that bases the moral assessment of actions on their intrinsic character must be in play, and this of course is ruled out by strict consequentialism.

I have elsewhere argued that this is a mistake.[7] Some single-principle versions of act-consequentialism allow for dilemmas, for situations in which, in the light of the principle, one cannot avoid wrongdoing. Thus consider the principle of utility as put forward in the 1789 original edition of Bentham's *An Introduction to the Principles of Morals and Legislation* (and retained in the 1823 version though implicitly qualified—or contradicted?—in footnote, by a different, and to us more familiar, version of the principle). Bentham says that the rightness or wrongness of an act depends on whether it promotes or opposes overall human happiness. This principle allows for dilemmas, because it seems in no way impossible for a person to be in a situation where whatever she does (including doing nothing) will in one way or another be harmful to overall human happiness.

I believe that it is from utilitarian moral dilemmas that we can best learn how to construct a plausible example of non-moral rational dilemma. The natural self-regarding rational analogue of the just mentioned example of utilitarian moral dilemma would be based on the single principle that an act is (self-regardingly) rational if and only if it contributes to—or at least doesn't decrease—the overall well-being, happiness, or preference-satisfaction of the agent. Such a principle would allow of rational dilemma if true, because where an agent cannot help but make his situation worse whatever he does, nothing he does will count as rational according to the principle, even if he chooses the least self-damaging option available to him. But the principle is not plausible and neither, as a form of utilitarianism, is the original Bentham principle that allows for dilemmas. Nevertheless, such principles do allow us to see that intrinsic non-consequentialistic characterizations need not figure in every set of principles that permits dilemmas. And more significantly for our present purposes, Bentham's original principle points to an area of common moral thinking that contemporary optimizing act-utilitarianism neglects, but his earlier form in some measure accommodates.

Many of the most plausible examples of common-sense

moral dilemmas involve someone having to choose who should be harmed and in what way, but having no choice but to do or permit harm to someone. And one can be morally anguished by being in such a position even if one sees one's way clearly as to how to minimize the amount of harm done. In certain situations the minimization of harm is incumbent on us, but we also seem positively bound not to do or allow any major harm. Sophie may well feel—and we may agree with her—that the sacrifice of her daughter is not morally justified by the fact that she had to sacrifice someone and the harm to her daughter is no greater than that of any alternative that was within her power. Ordinary morality, ordinary benevolence, ordinary parental care, seek not merely to minimize harm to children but to prevent them from suffering harm at all, and if in a given circumstance one will be a means to irreparable catastrophic harm to one of one's children no matter how one acts, one may still understandably feel guilty for what one has allowed to happen when one has finally made one's choice among evils. In some circumstances, the minimization of harm or choice of the lesser of evils may not involve one in actual wrongdoing, but in others, like Sophie's, an intuitive case can be made for saying that it does, and that fact indicates a place (yet another place) where optimizing utilitarian act-consequentialism diverges from common sense moral thinking, but where Bentham's original utilitarian principle, for all its implausibilities as a general criterion of right and wrong, comes closer to such thinking.[8]

I want to suggest at this point that something very similar can be maintained about our common sense thinking about rationality. The principle that it is rational to make a certain choice if and only if it does, or can be expected to do, good for the agent is certainly too broad and implausible, but there are occasions where the inevitable self-damage is so irreparable—so significant for or central to one's long-term prospects in life—that no choice available may seem rationally acceptable. Here is an example to illustrate such a possibility.

Consider a young man, living in the United States before the American entry into World War II, who has a strong interest in being a lawyer but an equally strong interest, persisting from student days, in archaeology. (The geopolitical and historical facts are now going to become largely imaginary.) The man has been drafted, and his army unit is due to be transferred to Cambodia in a few months' time. Having graduated from law school and passed the bar in his home state, he needs only to be sworn in as a member of the bar in order to be eligible for legal work when his unit is transferred abroad. But he chose this particular unit because he also wants to be near certain temples on which he would like to be able to do extended archaeological research. He needs to obtain permission from the Cambodian embassy in Washington in order to work at the temples (because the Cambodians insist that foreigners have their credentials verified in their home countries), but he expects to be able to go to Washington to get the permission before his unit leaves for Cambodia.

Suddenly the Japanese attack Pearl Harbor, and his unit's departure date is rescheduled for two days later. On the intervening day he has time either to attend a swearing-in ceremony for admission to the bar or to visit Washington to obtain clearance for his archaeological work, but not to do both. So whatever he does, the results for him will be highly unsatisfactory. If he gets his credentials checked in Washington, he will be able to pursue his archaeological work, but will for a number of years be restricted to peeling potatoes in the army, rather than developing his skills as a lawyer. What a waste! But if he becomes a lawyer and misses out on the archaeological research, then he will have missed a unique opportunity. He has a firm commitment to archaeology, but he will need to earn his living, after military service, in the law. Never again will he have the chance to do the kind of extended field work necessary to first-rate accomplishments in archaeology. So if he doesn't get a chance to work at the temples, he will rue and regret it the rest of his life. Again, what a waste!

The man himself may recognize all these difficulties and so realize that whatever he decides to do on the intervening day will result in an irreparable sacrifice of something enormously, centrally, important to him and to his conception of his own good. Whatever he chooses, it will be appropriate for him to have a profound and painful sense of dashed hopes, so in many ways his situation is analogous to Sophie's. Protecting her children is essential to Sophie's conception of herself as a decent caring person, and to sacrifice either child is, from her standpoint, to do something terrible, to sacrifice something essential to her moral self-esteem, to incur horrendous guilt.

Our man in the army will presumably not incur guilt for sacrificing his archaeological work or his legal work; but either choice will involve him in sacrificing something he considers essential to his personal development and well-being. His choice, whichever one he makes, will put a blight on a substantial portion of the rest of his life, and so afterwards he too can, and realistically must, feel he has done a terrible thing to himself. In him a sense of rue will be as appropriate, and as realistic, as Sophie's sense of guilt.[9] In common-sense terms, then, there is at least some reason to think that doing the best one can is not always sufficient to avoid morally or rationally unacceptable choice or action. It is not entirely clear, even in common-sense terms, what we should say about Sophie's choice; but the reasons that exist for saying she inevitably acted wrongly are paralleled by reasons for saying that the man in the army (through no prior rational fault) must sacrifice a part of his life and hopes that it cannot be rational of him to sacrifice. (If you think the would-be archaeologist/lawyer is expecting too much from life and ought to be contented—not rueful—if allowed to pursue either of his career choices to the fullest, then change the example. Imagine, instead, a desperately poor seventeenth-century Neapolitan boy offered the choice of a long, comfortable professional life as a soprano.)

But just as the idea of moral dilemma invariably evokes some opposition even among defenders of common-sense morality, there is something intuitively, or at least initially, repugnant in the idea of a rational dilemma. It is usually held, and it is natural to hold, that an intelligent person always has it within her power to figure out at least one rational course of action in any given situation, or at least that within any given practical context there is always at least one rational, reasonable course of action which it is in principle possible for a rational agent to discern.[10] So the idea that it may not be rational to optimize or maximize if in so doing one does (or expects to do) sufficient damage to one's life prospects or preferences has a purchase on some, but by no means all, of our common-sense intuitions about rational choice. (To the extent it represents a truth about practical rationality, we have encountered a new sort of restriction on rational optimizing/ maximizing.) Similarly, the possibility of moral dilemmas entails one kind of moral luck, and the idea of moral luck is offensive to at least one side of common moral thinking; but a fairly strong intuitive case can, nonetheless, be made in favor of viewing Sophie as acting wrongly even while doing the morally best she can (in circumstances she is not responsible for creating). This way of treating the case has, as I have said, a certain resonance with the earlier form of Bentham's principle of utility, but clearly it finds no foothold in standard optimizing (utilitarian) act-consequentialism, where it is taken to be perfectly sufficient for the rightness and moral acceptability of an act that it have consequences as impersonally good as those of any alternative, that it represent a least of evils.

However, I would like now to show that even a purely optimizing principle of utility leaves open the possibility of a certain kind of moral dilemma. At least, in principle, in certain situations it can be impossible to optimize utility, to perform an act with consequences at least as good as those of any other available act. And on contemporary versions of act-utilitarianism or act–consequentialism such a situation would constitute a dilemma.

II

But how is such a thing possible even in principle? Will there not always be some act with consequences better than or at least as good as those of all the other acts available to the agent? Not if the agent is capable of doing any of an infinite number of acts and no one of them is first or tied-first in the goodness of its consequences. Consider the following logically coherent science-fiction scenario (it may be possible to think of more mundane cases illustrating the same point but I have not been able to think of any). If, for any n, one can stand $1/n$th of an inch from a given wall and God will create n happy people (or add n happy days to the lives of people who are here already) if one stands $1/n$th of an inch away from that wall at a given time, then under various simplifying assumptions, any act one performs will have less good consequences than some other act one could have performed; no act one can perform at the time in question will be either best or tied-best and by the usual act-utilitarian criterion one will inevitably act wrongly. (In describing this case, I have referred to actual rather than expectable consequences, but nothing in our present discussion will turn on this distinction.)

So even under plausible contemporary interpretations of the principle of utility, moral dilemma is coherently imaginable, and this result may encourage us to look for analogous cases in which self-regarding rational dilemma is unavoidable. If situations are imaginable in which no action one can perform has as good overall consequences as any other action one can perform, is it not likewise possible to conceive of a case where no action a given individual can perform has optimal consequences for that very individual, a situation where the agent has no way to achieve what is best or tied-best (or most preference-satisfying) for herself, because, for any given act she performs, some alternative action is available, with better (or more preference-satisfying) consequences for herself?

This possibility does exist and it can be illustrated along the lines of our example of utilitarian/consequentialist moral dilemma. The examples of rational dilemma to be mentioned are purely hypothetical: they all involve unrealistic, or science-fictional, assumptions about human powers and opportunities. But they are nonetheless relevant to the issue of principle we are considering. If such rational dilemmas are distinctly conceivable, that will have important conceptual and philosophical implications for the way we understand practical rationality.

Imagine a special kind of fountain of youth. It emits life-and-happiness-giving rays and can work for a given person only once and at a certain precise moment. Depending how far from the fountain one is at the exact time when its rays bombard one, one will be given additional days of life and happiness. Assume further that one is capable of standing as close as one pleases to the fountain. For any n, one is capable of standing $1/n$th of an inch away from the fountain, and if one stays at $1/n$th of an inch away one will receive n extra days of happiness (if one touches the fountain all bets are off). In such a case, any proximity one chooses will be less than some other proximity one could have chosen, and so however many happy days one adds to one's life, one could have added many more—equally many, twice as many, and so forth. If one is aware of the above circumstances and uniformly prefers or is better off with more rather than fewer happy days,[11] then an optimizing or preference-maximizing model of rationality will say that one inevitably performs some act of standing at a certain distance from the fountain such that there was a better act to perform: for example, one stands at $1/n$th of an inch from the machine, and it would have been better to stand $1/2n$th of an inch from the machine. In other words, one has more reason on balance to stand $1/2n$th inches away than to stand $1/n$th inches away and so for any action one performs one had more reason to perform some alternative in one's power. But if it is not rational to do one thing, when one has more reason to perform some alternative, when it would have been (a) better (choice) to have performed some definitely available alternative, then one has, inevitably, failed to act rationally in the circumstances just mentioned. And so we have described a rational dilemma for preference-maximizing and for optimizing (including good-maximizing) conceptions of extramoral practical rationality. But not just for them. Even someone who commonsensically accepts the idea of rational satisficing or of rational restrictions on optimizing is likely to see the above case as involving a rational dilemma.

Those moderate individuals for whom reasons like "that's much more than I need" are reasons for not choosing what would be best for themselves often choose what is less than best for themselves, but on such occasions, according to their lights, the balance of reasons favors making such a choice; so they can hold that it is best for them to choose or do what will result in less good for themselves (though note the ambiguity in "best for them"). So too the person who, for instance, lacks an interest in optimizing because she is thoroughly satisfied with her present condition need not regard her failure to optimize as a failure to do what it is most rational, or best, for her to do: optimizing may actually count as an irrational option by her lights.

Thus our previous discussion of common-sense rationality in no way suggests that it can be rational to do an act not favored by the balance of an agent's reasons, an act less than rationally best by the agent's lights: the point has been, rather, that a non-optimizing choice may be seen as rationally best and an optimizing (or preference-maximizing) one as rationally unacceptable (and less than best). And to the extent we continue to maintain that a rational choice must not be less than the best choice available, I think our fountain-of-youth example will count as a dilemma even for those who deny optimizing and maximizing models of rational choice. The example naturally invites an optimizing or maximizing model of rationality, or, to put things more precisely, it represents an occasion where none of our previously mentioned reasons against optimizing and preference-maximization seems applicable.[12] Satisfaction with less than immortality, or with a shorter rather than a longer life, is not part of our ordinary conception of moderation or modesty of desire: the moderate individual may be indifferent (at a certain point) to more happiness in the sense of greater or more intense happiness, but no element of moderation attaches to a willingness to allow one's life to end sooner rather than later.[13] (Perhaps it is irrational for us humans not to *accept* our unavoidable mortality, but it hardly follows that we would have reasons of moderation, or of any other kind, to reject immortality if it were ever on offer.) Moreover, none of the rational restrictions on optimizing—or preference-maximizing—seems applicable in the fountain-of-youth example, so it is very difficult to block the move from "choice with better—or more preference-satisfying—results for oneself" to "better choice." It would appear that for any distance an individual chooses to stand from the fountain, there are other closer positions which he had more reason to choose. And since it seems self-evidently not to be rational to make a given choice when a better, more rationally supported choice is clearly available, we appear to face a rational dilemma, even without holding optimizing or preference-maximizing views of rational choice.

Of course, we could easily evade the dilemma if, with Bernard Williams,[14] we held that immortality was not a good thing and attempted to infer that there was some (vaguely specifiable) finite length of life beyond which it is worth no one's while—and no one would want—to live. But such a way out would be as paradoxical as the idea of rational dilemma itself, which seems fairly to force itself upon us in our attempt to describe the example we have been focusing on. If one is really pleased at the prospect of n additional happy days of life, one will presumably prefer and have reason to prefer $2n$ additional days, and it seems undeniable not only that the person who stands at $1/n$th inch away and gets n extra happy days would have been better off if she had chosen to stand $1/2n$th inches away, but that she would have done better to stand at $1/2n$th inches away. She was capable of standing at the latter distance and there was reason for her to stand at that distance rather than at the distance she actually chose (she has no reason of moderation to be reluctant or indifferent about choosing to stand closer and have the longer life). So whatever she chooses to do, it would on the balance of reasons have been better for her to choose otherwise.

Moreover, even if in this case the existence of dilemma depends on an assumption about the goodness of (or a preference for) indefinitely long pleasurable existence, it is possible to construct a rather similar example requiring no such assumption. Imagine that God has condemned some wine connoisseur to an infinite life with only as finitely much of his favorite wine, Chateau Effete, as he asks for on a certain occasion. How many bottles of Chateau Effete should he ask for as a consolation for the unpleasant tedium of his largely wineless immortality? Since no finite amount is an immoderate quantity (or represents insatiable greed) when consumed over infinite time, the man will have reason to specify as large a finite amount as possible; and whatever amount he actually specifies, there will be (more) reason for him to choose some larger amount.

Practical rational dilemma, whether from an optimizing, a preference-maximizing or a common-sense rational standpoint, thus seems inevitable in the case of our wine connoisseur, and given some rather plausible assumptions about the desirability of indefinitely long (happy) life, in the fountain-of-youth case as well. Even if we may wish to hold that it can be self-regardingly rational to choose less than the best (results) for oneself, it seems not to be rational to make a given choice when, as in our examples, a better, a more rationally supported, choice is clearly available.

But there is another possibility. Even granting that whatever a given person chooses, she had some other better choice, we may still discern degrees of rationality in the cases we have described. Clearly, it would be irrational in our first example for someone to stand only a quarter of an inch from the "fountain of youth" (or, in our second example, for the connoisseur to ask for only five bottles of Chateau Effete). To stand one billionth of an inch away from the fountain would be a much better thing to do, and perhaps there are degrees of proximity that it would be rational (not irrational) to choose, even though it would have been better, more rational, to have chosen some even greater degree of proximity. In other words, it may be possible for an act (choice) not to count as irrational or bad—perhaps even to count as rationally acceptable and good—though it is less than ideally rational, less than the best available.

III

But such a way out of rational dilemma involves one in denying an assumption that, as far as I am aware, has always been accepted as obvious by philosophers discussing practical rationality: the assumption (roughly) that it is irrational—or at least not rational—to act in a given way when one believes there is some alternative action which one has, on balance, more reason to perform, which it would be better (and the sense of "better" here is in no way limited to moral considerations) to perform. In discussing earlier whether satisficing was a form of weakness of will we took note of this assumption in the work of Donald Davidson, but it is taken for granted, as far as I can tell, by everyone who has dealt with practical reason and practical rationality.[15]

Taking it for granted amounts to a denial of the possibility of rational supererogation. The morally supererogatory exists, we know, if some moral or non-immoral acts are morally less good than some of their alternatives. For an act is morally superogatory if it is morally better than some alternative that would not have been wrong. However, even if common-sense morality seems to make abundant room for super-erogation, there are moral theories which rule it out. Act-consequentialists and act-utilitarians, for example, rank acts according to their consequences and nowadays typically hold that right actions must have optimal consequences relative to their alternatives, and thus be better than (or as good as) any of their alternatives. So for such a utilitarian no act can be right unless there is no alternative open to the agent which is mor-ally better than it. But this is not in general true of moral views, and common sense allows for the moral acceptability of behavior that has morally superior, for example, heroic and saintly, alternatives.

However, the topic of rational supererogation has not expe-rienced such division of opinion, or perhaps we should say that there has simply never been such a topic as rational supererogation, because everyone—from optimizing/maxi-mizing theorists to defenders of Aristotelian ideas about ra-tionality—has taken it for granted that it is not rationally acceptable to do one thing when from a rational standpoint it would be better for one to do something else. Perhaps we have motive and reason to question this assumption, if we wish to avoid allowing for certain rational dilemmas, but the optimiz-ing or maximizing theorist of rationality, like the optimizing moral consequentialist, may in fact have no reason to deny the possibility of dilemmas once she sees how she is committed to them. Philosophers have objected to the extent of moral luck involved in moral dilemmas, but (utilitarian) act-consequentialism is from the start up to its ears in luck and has, in any case, its own special ways of detaching judgments of wrongdoing from blameworthiness or culpability: even if an act is wrong, it may not be culpable, because, on consequentialist grounds, it would be wrong to blame or punish the agent for the wrongdoing. (For example, on optimizing act-consequentialism it was probably wrong for Hitler's mother not to have killed him. But it might do, or have done, harm to blame her for her actions, and a consequentialist may wish to conclude that her actions shouldn't be morally criticized and are therefore not blameworthy.) Now, adherents of an optimizing or preference-maximizing view of rationality can maintain a similar distinction between what is rational and what it is rational, or moral, to criticize; so the "retreat" into rational supererogation may not have much to recommend it apart from intuitive considerations that weigh less with defenders of maximizing and optimizing, presumably, than with adherents of a common-sense view of rationality or morality (and perhaps with some Aristotelians).

However, the unintuitiveness, at least initially, of the idea of rational dilemma may give the more commonsensically minded a reason to make room for rational supererogation. If we allow that an act may be rational (rationally permissible) or be a good act to perform, even though more reason supports, and it would be better to perform, some alternative, then we may be able to avoid the infinitistic dilemmas described above. Furthermore, once we have been given a motive for questioning the assumption that rationality requires doing what is rationally best (or what is rationally not less than the best),[16] we may begin to notice intuitive reasons for questioning that assumption that are quite independent of any felt need to rule out rational dilemmas.

What I have in mind is perhaps best introduced via recent discussions of *akrasia* (weakness of will). Unlike most discussions of akrasia, Donald Davidson's "How Is Weakness of the Will Possible?" makes it abundantly clear that more than two alternatives can be at issue in cases of akrasia. According to Davidson, if act *b* is believed better than act *a* and the agent chooses *b*, she is not off the akratic hook if there is some further action *c* which she thinks is better than *b*. But I think we can produce some good reasons to doubt whether this must always be the case. In certain complex cases of what must on standard accounts be regarded as akrasia, it is not unnatural or strained to speak of degrees of rationality, to regard less than ideal or maximum rationality as rational enough, as rationally acceptable.

Let us consider two examples. A man and his wife have quarrelled and in a fit of pique the wife has gone back to her mother's threatening to stay there indefinitely. The man is disconcerted, hurt, angry; he feels greater and greater frustration as the situation drags on, but he believes his wife will come back to him and hopes to be able to help bring this about. However, right now, his wife being still away, he is at a party and one of the female guests begins to flirt with him, indeed suggests her sexual availability, and the man is tempted. But he believes it would be morally and prudentially better for him not to get physically involved with her in any way. He also believes that it would be possible, though very difficult, for him entirely to resist her advances. In his state of frustration and anxiety he gives in to the blandishments to a certain extent, engages in what used to be called "heavy necking." Somehow the lesser physical intimacy takes the edge off his frustration and actually helps him resist greater intimacy. But he may know, and we may assume, that most men in his position would have completely succumbed to the blandishments, and, in particular, that most men who had gone as far as he has would have gone all the way. So although he has not done what he deems best, has fallen short of what his own conception of ideal rationality dictates in the circumstances, his own feelings after the fact may be more those of relief and even pride, than of shame or regret. He may feel that although going as far as he did was not the best available action, it was not, in the circumstances, a bad thing for him to do.[17] What he did was not ideally rational, but neither, he may feel, was what he did simply unacceptable: although it demonstrated some weakness of will, it demonstrated considerable strength of will as well.[18] If he exerted more rational control than we can reasonably expect of most people, then perhaps his act of going-as-far-as-he-did-but-no-farther is rational enough so that it would be a mistake, in common-sense or intuitive terms, simply to deny its rational acceptability.

Take another example. A man is angry at his boss and believes (for good reasons we needn't enter into) that it would be in his own interest, and on the whole a good thing, to tell the boss off when they next meet. He believes it would be best to do so in a loud enough voice so that everyone in the office will know what is happening. But both he and his fellow employees have long been intimidated by the boss, and the employee knows it will be difficult to stand up to the boss and tell him what he thinks, and even more difficult (though not impossible) to do so in the loud and angry tones he thinks most appropriate. When the time comes to confront the boss, he manages with considerable effort to speak his mind, but allows himself to be intimidated to the extent of not daring to do so loudly and angrily; and indeed from a rational standpoint and relative to the man's own values, it would have been better for him to speak angrily to the boss than to express his opinion in conversational tones. But the latter may have been difficult enough so that on the whole the man is more proud than ashamed at his performance. Even though his performance may be less than the best that lay within his power, it may be good enough for him and for us not to regard it as rationally unacceptable. So again we seem to have an intuitively plausible rational analogue of what common-sense morality requires for supererogation. Moral supererogation is possible if there can be (extended) action which is less than ideal, less good than it could be, but which is nonetheless good enough not to count as immoral or wrong. And our above examples seem, analogously, to involve less than ideally rational choice and action that need not be regarded as rationally unacceptable or impermissible.

There are two sorts of reasons, then, for admitting the notions of rational supererogation and of less-than-ideal practical rationality: the linguistic and phenomenological *naturalness* of conceiving certain examples in those terms, and whatever desire we may have to avoid rational dilemma. And we must now consider how the idea of supererogation can help us to evade dilemma in the fountain-of-youth case (or the case of accumulating Chateau Effete).

It seems outright irrational for someone with the powers we have assumed to stand at certain distances, say ¼th of an inch, away from the science-fiction fountain of youth,[19] but how much closer does one have to choose to stand in order for one's choice no longer to count as rationally unacceptable? In the supererogation-friendly examples of yielding partially to sexual temptation and of failure to speak loudly to the boss, the agent accomplishes most, the most important part, of what ideal rationality requires, but it would be difficult to apply this notion to the fountain-of-youth case, where one inevitably gains only an (infinitesimally) small fraction of the number of extra happy days one had reason, and the power, to obtain. In order to treat such examples as dilemma-free, we must borrow another feature of our "natural" paradigms of rational supererogation.

The performance of the man who does everything but speak loudly may count as rationally acceptable, because of the great difficulty of doing (rationally) better than he has done. (It may be unreasonable, for example, to expect others to do as well as he has done.) And we can similarly imagine in the fountain-of-youth case that, even though one can stand at any finite close distance, still the closer the distance the more difficult it would be to summon the concentration and the intelligence required to stand at that distance. The difficulty of standing at closer and closer distances thus approaches the limits of the agent's power and skill. In that case, an agent who through great effort and concentration chose to stand at a distance so near that it would have been very difficult (for him or for anyone else) to choose to stand any nearer, may count as having chosen in a rationally acceptable way.[20] And we can see how to avoid the admission of infinitistic rational dilemmas by allowing for rational supererogation, for a gap between rationality and ideal rationality.[21]

On the other hand, someone—even someone who finds the idea of rational dilemma initially objectionable—may regard our "natural" examples of rational supererogation as more convincing than the above attempt to avoid dilemmas, and so end up accepting both rational supererogation and rational dilemmas. But the issues widen at this point, because what one wants to say about rational dilemmas and supererogation is understandably influenced by what one wants to say about moral dilemmas and supererogation. There is a long ethical tradition of drawing analogies between rationality and morality, and this tendency, and the fact that the usual direction of influence has been from conceptions of rationality to moral views or theories, may serve to explain some features of recent and traditional moral theory and suggest some possibilities for the future.

If rational dilemmas can be supported, the case for moral dilemmas may well gain in strength. But, perhaps more significantly, if we allow for rational supererogation (doing so, in part, to avoid rational dilemma), then the case for moral supererogation may also be strengthened. Given the desire to base morality on an ideal or model of rationality, it has sometimes seemed a strength of optimizing (utilitarian) act-consequentialism that it resembles the presently dominant optimizing and maximizing theories of rational choice in ruling out supererogation. But if rational supererogation is accepted, then the supererogation-permitting aspect of common-sense morality may be reinforced, and the way is also opened to those earlier mentioned satisficing act-consequentialist theories that allow for moral supererogation by making it permissible to produce merely good enough consequences. (For act-consequentialists, an optimific act is morally better than any non-optimific alternative.)

Thus issues concerning rational supererogation are of crucial import to the understanding of the nature and rational status of different moral theories, and we shall have a great deal more to say about the ways in which this is so, after completing our general outline of common-sense practical rationality and its relation to the received view of rational choice. For now, we must push on with the task of understanding ordinary rationality, and the present chapter has laid the groundwork for an important further step.

We have already described some requirements of ordinary practical rationality that parallel those of common-sense deontological morality. But we have not mentioned the agent-relative (or agent-centered) *permissions* of common-sense morality, permissions to pursue whatever projects or commitments one wishes even when doing so does not serve overall optimality. On our ordinary view, it is not immoral to pursue (innocent) desires and plans even when it would be morally better to sacrifice them in the name of impersonal good. And a thoroughgoing parallelism between common-sense morality and rationality would require the existence of rational permissions to seek less than the best for oneself even when it would be more rational to pursue one's own greatest good.

Our earlier discussion of satisficing moderation and of restrictions on optimizing did not give us such a rational analogue of ordinary morality, since it was not held that the moderate satisficer was rational, but less rational than she would have been had she optimized. A parallel to ordinary morality would have to be a case where one acts rationally but would have been more rational to act otherwise, and would thus have to allow for rational supererogation. The defense heretofore (at least from a common-sense standpoint) of rational supererogation does yield some sort of parallel with common morality's agent-relative permissions; but in fact closer analogues can be found, and I shall be exploring these in the next chapter.

· 6 ·

The Rational Permissions of "Fractional Prudence"

Sidgwick's insistence on the analogy between interpersonal considerations and intertemporal considerations within the life of a single individual has had a creative influence on recent ethical theory.[1] This analogy can help us to locate some of our best examples of rational permissions that are analogous with common-sense moral permissions to pursue personal concerns and projects in an impersonally non-optimific fashion.

I

As I indicated earlier, common moral permissions to lead one's life non-optimifically involve elements both of permission and supererogation. One has permission to act non-optimifically where some alternative would be morally better, and supererogatory, because (closer to being) optimific. Thus according to moral common sense, the person who devotes herself to a lucrative professional career in medicine when she could have done more overall good by going off to help the sick and starving in Africa does what is morally permissible, but not particularly praiseworthy; the alternative (extended) action of helping the needy in Africa is morally better and so counts as supererogatory. A parallel in the area of self-regarding reason would require us to find examples where something was rationally permitted, yet less rational than some alternative which in that case would count as rationally supererogatory. Indeed, we have looked at some such examples in the last chapter. But in order to put those examples in proper perspective, I believe we must invoke the familiar parallel between the moral/interpersonal and the individualistically rational/intertemporal and make use of some new examples that allow us to take full advantage of that parallelism.

Ordinary morality's permissions to pursue one's own innocent concerns or projects are, at least in the most obvious cases, permissions to favor oneself, the agent, over other people, even though it would be morally better and supererogatory to treat others more equally with oneself (or put their interests ahead of one's own). We naturally tend to favor ourselves over others, and common-sense morality allows us to do so within limits while at the same time recommending or preferring a more even-handed or altruistic approach.[2] The self-regarding sphere includes an analogous tendency to favor pressing present desires or feelings and one's own nearer future over one's remote future and the desires that (one knows) will exist in it. But to the large majority of philosophers who have discussed practical rationality this widespread tendency to give greater weight to present desires, and so forth, has seemed a clear example of irrationality. C. I. Lewis, who makes use of the convenient expression "fractional prudence" to describe a greater concern for one's nearer future, treats such concern as clearly irrational, and countless others have rejected favoritism toward present desires and the nearer future as forms of irrational "time preference."[3]

Yet as Lewis notes, and Parfit has recently reminded us,[4] at least one philosopher treats the preference for the near future, and so forth, as a *requirement* of practical rationality. In *An Introduction to the Principles of Morals and Legislation* Bentham tells us that the soonness of a pleasure affects its value (for us), while separately noting that the likelihood of a pleasure affects its value, so it seems plausible to interpret Bentham as saying that we should be less concerned about our remote future quite independently of the greater uncertainty that may attach to it.[5] And whereas Lewis strongly disagrees with Bentham so understood, Parfit is somewhat sympathetic, though a discussion of his reasons for being so would take us far from our main task.

But one thing common to Parfit, Lewis, and others—and bearing essentially on the thesis of the present chapter—is the fact that they treat the alternatives "preference for the near future is a rational requirement" and "preference for the near future is irrational" as exhausting the possibilities.[6] There is room, however, for another view. Even granting that it is *more rational* to treat the times of one's future equally (except as discounted for uncertainty), it does not follow, and one may deny, that it is always less than rational to give some preference to the near, e.g., to present impulses. In that case one regards the widespread preference for the near future as analogous with what is commonly believed, in morality, about the natural preference for oneself, and the very possibility of such an analogy makes it surprising that in discussions of preference for the near, the view giving rise to the analogy has not been mentioned. The explanation may lie in the tendency to dissociate rationality from any sort of supererogation. But we have already seen enough support for the idea of practical rational supererogation to encourage us to look more closely at this third possible view about preference for the near future, and what most forcefully favors it and thus recommends a form of rational supererogation differing from any I have mentioned so far, is the fact that it comes closer to common sense than either Bentham's or Lewis's view of fractional prudence.

Of course, people in the course of their lives frequently do give preference to the nearer future, and to the pressure of present fear and desire, thereby incurring an overall less satisfactory course of their lives. But Bentham seemingly holds that such preference is rationally *required*, that we sometimes *should* prefer a lesser nearer good to a greater later good that would result in an overall better life, and surely that is not the view of common sense. (Common-sense doesn't even hold that the tendency to prefer the nearer future is *more* rational than the tendency to give equal weight to all times present and future.)

Is our common-sense opinion, then, that the tendency to prefer the near is simply irrational? I think not. It seems much more in tune with ordinary thinking to hold, rather, that a tendency to give some preference to the nearer future, while not ideally or entirely rational—not as rational as a temporally more neutral attitude—is not necessarily irrational or rationally unacceptable either. In other words, common-sense rationally *tolerates* a certain amount of favoritism toward the present and immediate future, and this is analogous to the way in which common sense morality tolerates, but does not recommend, the giving of greater weight to one's own concerns and projects.

Parfit says that many of us would intuitively not regard it as irrational for people to experience a sense of relief when a bad event is postponed or to feel mounting excitement when some good event approaches the present. But those intuitions, while raising doubts about the irrationality of preferring the nearer future, more clearly favor the view that such a preference is not irrational than they favor the stronger, Benthamite view that Parfit tentatively supports. And even Lewis, who, like Parfit, does not consider the possibility of rational supererogation in discussing our attitudes toward future times, sometimes uses language that helps to give that possibility a foothold. He says, for example, that the preference for the nearer "expresses an attitude which humans do tend to take, instead of acting wholly from rational grounds." But the phrase "wholly from rational grounds" clearly suggests the possibility of acting partly from rational grounds and of doing so in such a way that the part or fraction of (ideal) rationality is sufficiently large to render it inappropriate to characterize such action as less than rational. Fractional prudence—when the fraction assignable to prudence is large enough in proportion to the fraction assignable to impulse or desire—need not be treated simply as imprudence, or as rationally unacceptable, just as fractional altruism may not in common-sense terms count as morally wrong when the fraction of concern for others is sufficiently large in relation to concern for oneself.[7] And if this rough parallel is correct, then, according to our common-sense rational standards or intuitions, it is rationally acceptable that ideally rational equal concern for present and future times should be attenuated to some extent by occurrent desires, by prerational or animal impulse, just as we intuitively find it morally acceptable that a morally ideal or supererogatory evenhandedness as between others and ourselves (and apart from special obligations incurred to others) should be attenuated to some extent by our self-regarding rationality and self-regarding impulses.

We therefore seem to have a parallelism between common-sense moral supererogations involving the transcendence of morally permissible limitations on our concern for others and common-sense rational supererogations involving the transcendence of rationally permissible limitations on our concern with remote times in our own future. Quelling present impulse in favor of one's own greater long-term good may be rationally supererogatory in much the same way that quelling selfish impulse in the name of the general good is ordinarily considered to be morally supererogatory. And in the light of this close analogy, more perhaps can be said to illuminate the rational supererogations spoken of in the last chapter. The supererogations we discussed there are not based in any particular attitude toward or behavior with respect to time, and so do not instantiate the powerful familiar analogy between the intertemporal and interpersonal. Nonetheless, they have something important in common with the time-based forms of rational supererogation we have just been describing. The latter involve overcoming our natural, but from a common-sense standpoint acceptable preference for the nearer future and, most particularly, involve overcoming our tendency to be influenced by the strength of present impulse rather than by the thought of later goods or impulses. Our present fear of the dentist may make us happy to postpone visiting her even when we know that at the time to which the visit has been postponed our fear and discomfort, given our deteriorating condition, are likely to be even greater.

The cases of possible supererogation discussed in the last chapter also involved the overcoming of prerational or non-rational impulse. But if, for example, one succeeds in over-coming the fear of speaking up to one's boss, one's superiority to someone who gives in to such fear is not a function of one's having a more rational attitude *toward time*. As I stated the example, it is true, of course, that the person who doesn't dare to speak loudly to the boss believes that it would later benefit him and his co-workers if he had spoken loudly; but clearly this sort of example doesn't in any essential way depend on such a relation to future time. We can imagine that the sole (and valid) aim of the protesting worker is that someone should tell the boss what he thinks of him while simulta-neously allowing his fellow workers to be in on this unprece-dented rebellion; and here the aim is focused on the immediate future. The person may not particularly care whether his fellow workers remember that he told the boss off; and the choice may simply be between giving in to an impulse relating to the immediate future and doing the best thing one can do in the immediate future. The issue of how fully rational one is going to be in choosing among one's options may involve no differential attitudes toward future times.

Still, the person who doesn't overcome all his fear of the

boss and is by his own and our lights less rational than he had hoped to be may be more rational than he had feared he would be and so is possibly not to be accused of having acted less than rationally. There is an opposition between impulse and what is thought best and most rational, but rationality may nonetheless be held willing to accommodate less than total victories over impulse. One may be rationally permitted to do less than the rationally ideal or best. Such cases do not, however, essentially raise issues of fractional prudence, but most fundamentally and most simply concern fractional levels of total or optimal rationality concerning (present) alternatives. And by the same token, not every morally permissible, less than morally optimal, action need be an example of fractional altruism: certain forms of conscientiousness may be more than common-sense morality requires, but bear no essential relation to the well-being of others.

II

In all the cases of rational supererogation we have discussed so far, ideal or circumstantially optimal rationality is thought to be subject to attenuation by impulse, desire, or fear, without leading to irrationality *simpliciter*. We are subject to strong impulses untamed, as it were, by our rational values, and our views about practical rationality may recognize and give in to this kind of animal substrate in us by allowing for compromises between the impulses and purely rational values. But the picture needs to be broadened at this point to accommodate some forms of common-sense rational supererogation our previous discussion ignores.

Our treatment of rational supererogation has been too narrow, in part because we have so far been drawing parallels with the narrow view of moral supererogation and permission that has predominated in the recent literature of ethics. Most recent moral philosophers have conceived supererogation as involving the favoring of impersonal or moral aims over our own strong personal concerns and commitments, and of course rational supererogation is analogously understood as an overcoming of strong impulses. But the permissions of common-sense morality are in fact much broader than this picture can accommodate. Recent defenses of agent-centered permissions to act and live non-optimifically (and non-supererogatorily) often stress the unfairness or unreasonableness of the (optimizing) act-consequentialist's requirement that agents sacrifice their deepest projects and commitments when this is necessary to the production of (impersonally judged) best consequences. Other critics say that the act-consequentialist standard of right action constitutes a (moral) assault on the integrity of most agents, meaning, roughly, on their deepest sense of their own identity, and, again, this criticism is thought to support the moral permissibility of pursuing (innocent) personal projects and commitments. From that standpoint, the morally free sacrifice of one's actual projects and commitments in the name of overall optimality may then be viewed as morally supererogatory.

However, as I have argued at length elsewhere,[8] such an account of where act-consequentialism goes wrong unduly narrows the scope of our common-sense permissions to pursue non-optimific careers, commitments, projects, concerns, desires, and so forth. Focus, for the moment, just on careers and career-related projects. Is someone who is not yet even trying to decide on a career to be forbidden to follow a career, say, in teaching just because at this point such a restriction doesn't interfere with his current sense of identity or projects? We do not usually think a person's moral permission to pursue a certain career is conditional on his having chosen or particularly caring about that career. And even when someone has chosen a particular career, the permission to opt out, to choose a different career, seems available.[9] I was permitted to go into art before I chose philosophy, and that permission didn't dry up when I chose philosophy and lost all interest in a career in art.

Yet the persisting moral permission to go into art cannot be accounted for or justified on the usual grounds that it would shatter my integrity, or unfairly thwart my career and my projects, if I were forbidden to pursue a career in art. If any infringement is involved in requiring me not to pursue art, it is not an infringement of what I am most deeply identified with or concerned about, but of my moral autonomy, as we commonly conceive it, to pursue any innocent project whatever. The common-sense permissibility of my marrying Clara or pursuing a career in art exists independently of any desire or plan on my part to take advantage of such permissions, and in that sense our ordinary moral permissions to do less than the morally best include permissions that cannot be understood as (justified) concessions to our individualistic concerns or self-regarding preferences. I am at this moment permitted to drop philosophy even if that would involve a sacrifice of integrity and of my own good that cannot be justified on grounds of impersonal optimality.[10] Someone who would choose to thwart or ignore his own current interests and projects is typically seen as irrational or stupid, not as immoral, so ordinary morality differs from typical act-consequentialism in making a concession not only to rational self-interest but to possible non-optimific actions which do not further and may even thwart the agent's conception of his own good.

Roughly, then, we may say that ordinary morality makes moral allowance for certain "positive" elements in personal life, that is, for the presumptively rational pursuit of individual projects, concerns, and desires, but also accommodates certain possible failures of individualistic rationality. Both sorts of permission can be subsumed under the idea of moral autonomy or freedom. Intuitively, we are morally free to act rationally (but non-optimifically) in the pursuit of our goals and well-being and also to act irrationally (but again non-optimifically) against, or independently of, our actual goals or well-being. And I believe a similar split exists among our common-sense *rational* permissions. In order to see why, however, we need to consider a new class of examples; the sphere of *rational* permissions (and of concomitant rational supererogations) is much wider than we have yet acknowledged.

When we are lazy, we have, presumably, a desire to do nothing, or an aversion to work or other effortful activities, that can overwhelm our view of what would be best, most rational, for us to do. Laziness thus has its own force and (intentional) focus or aim, and in those respects differs from a phenomenon that may externally resemble it: the wasting, or frittering away, of time. The wasting of time is not typically brought about by a desire to waste time; and the idea of frittering away one's time implies that no single impulse or aim governs one's actions or behavior. Paradigmatically, someone who wastes or fritters away time lacks strong intentional direction or is subject to conflicting desires that she fails coherently to resolve. So wasting time reflects a kind of internal indefiniteness or disorder that distinguishes it not only from laziness but also from *killing* time. Someone who kills time in order to escape boredom may very well do so out of a strong desire to kill time and escape boredom: a single desire or set of related desires may govern his actions. But the wasting of time typically lacks these features. (A team that deliberately runs out the clock in a football game may be said to be deliberately wasting time; but I have some doubts about whether this description is accurate. Perhaps what they are doing is running out the clock while deliberately trying to make it seem to the referee and others as if they are merely wasting a bit of time here and there rather than deliberately running out the clock. "My purpose is to waste time" sounds odder to me than "my purpose is to kill time;" but even if one can deliberately waste time, there is another non-deliberate form of behavior that can properly be called time-wasting and that is the main focus of our present discussion.)

The wasting or frittering away of time involves, then, a kind of internal *anomie* or disorder, involves behavior not governed by any system of organized aims. Let me bring this home with an example. Someone is dressing in order to go to work: he puts on his shirt and then starts to wonder whether another, favorite shirt of his has come back from the cleaners. He looks through some drawers and, finding the shirt, goes back to dressing. Then he sees a newspaper in the corner of the bedroom and decides that that makes the room look untidy and unattractive. So he goes over and picks it up, but before he has time to put it in the wastebasket, he decides he is being awfully finicky; so he puts the newspaper back where it was and continues dressing. The man has already looked out the window to see whether it is raining, but at this point he takes one further, unnecessary look. And so it goes.

I think this man's behavior is similar to almost everyone's behavior much of the time and that he is not, in common-sense terms, acting irrationally. The man is presumably not killing time out of boredom; nor does he seem particularly lazy, for he is very active in his disorganized way. Rather, he acts seriatim from a number of momentary aims or velleities that bear no relation to his desire to get dressed for work or to any other overarching purpose. Such an individual fritters away time during the course of deliberately getting dressed for work—during the course of pursuing a rational purpose—so he is not just wasting time; he is wasting time while realizing a goal that (in a minor way) advances his own good. Are we going to say that such a person acts irrationally during the course of getting dressed? I don't intuitively see why we have to or should want to.

The man described may waste some time in useless activities, but he may nonetheless achieve his overall purpose of getting dressed efficiently enough so that his disorganized behavior, while falling short of ideal rationality, is not to be thought of as simply irrational. It may just not be reasonable to expect people to organize their time better than he does. So even if we think the man could make or could have made a better use of his time, we may still find his behavior so normal and tolerable as to be unwilling to consider it rationally unacceptable.

In that case, we shall not be withholding our criticism because we see some instrumental value, some form of instrumental rationality, in the time wasting. Aristotle and certain utilitarians have recommended rest and recreation as enabling us to recoup our strength and enthusiasm for further virtuous or optimific activity. And the wasting of time may also enable one to store energy and enthusiasm for valuable tasks. But our common-sense belief that the man of our example is sufficiently rational in his behavior need not be based on any assumption that his time-wasting helps him to conserve or restore energy for important tasks. Such a view, for one thing, would lead us in the direction of thinking that the man has a reason to waste time, but we can stipulate that the man of our example doesn't need to conserve energy and could make better use of his time, and in that case we can still plausibly deny that his behavior is less than rational—even if it is less rational than it might otherwise have been. This assessment will then make room for a rationally supererogatory efficiency, or husbanding of energies, that involves less frittering away of time than most of us are subject to.

In common-sense terms, then, there seem to be two very different kinds of rational permissions to do less than the rational best. We are sometimes rationally allowed to act on certain pressing desires and impulses even though such action is less rational than some other action available to us—where some of these desires express a favoritism toward the nearer future, but others do not. However, common sense also rationally tolerates a certain amount of time wasting, of behavior serving no particular desire of impulse, but attributable, instead, to an *absence* of focused intentionality, to internal disorder or *anomie*. When we prefer a nearer smaller pleasure to a greater later one and this, though not optimally rational, is considered rationally acceptable, we are being permitted to give in to an intentionally focused positive psychological force. But the common-sense permission to fritter a certain amount of time away (whether it holds only within the context of larger purposes or holds independently of such purposes) is not an accommodation, by practical reason, to something that opposes ideal rationality with its own forceful prerational intentionality; it is, rather, an accommodation to a certain less than ideally rational lack of coherent intentionality (absence of orderly desire). Such disorganization or *anomie* can causally interfere with the most efficient possible fulfillment of our desires and purposes; but that is not its purpose, and in fact it makes no sense to assume that someone who wastes time in the way I have been describing has any overall purpose in doing so.

Common-sense rationality's toleration for impulses, fears, and desires favoring the nearer future (to a certain extent) is very aptly described as a toleration for some level or amount of fractional prudence. But the toleration extended to disorderly, overall aimless time-wasting is perhaps more properly called a toleration for *fractional or fractionalized impulse*, since in such cases there is no definite, focused, effectual impulse or set of impulses at work, and we find only the play of momentary, fragmentary, unrelated impulses or velleities.

It should be fairly clear now, finally, that the two basic kinds of common-sense rational permissions described here—and their attendant rational supererogations—run fairly closely parallel to the two kinds of supererogation-allowing moral permissions we have also mentioned. Common-sense morality permits less than morally ideal or optimal behavior stemming from an agent's strong attachment to some conception of his own good, but it likewise accommodates less than morally (or rationally) optimal behavior not governed by the agent's conception of his own good (our common-sense permissions to act irrationally and self-thwartingly falling within this latter category).[11] And by the same token, common-sense practical rationality allows for less than rationally optimal behavior that stems from some particular strong impulse or desire and also for less than rationally optimal behavior not governed by any single or efficacious impulse or desire.

But of course our description of these analogous sets of permissions does not settle the issue of whether common sense is correct to assume they exist. The fact that common-sense moral permissions are neatly paralleled by common-sense rational ones may do something to support the whole set of such permissions and perhaps also common-sense ethics more generally, but I would like to leave further discussion of the validity of common-sense views till our final chapter.

In drawing analogies between common-sense rational and moral permissions, we have highlighted ways in which certain supererogation-allowing aspects of common-sense rationality contrast with a personally *optimizing* model of rational choice. But *preference-maximizing* models of rational choice also do not allow for rational supererogation, and it should be clear that our common-sense ideas about rational supererogation are simply incompatible with any preference-maximizing view. To be sure, when someone gives in to present desire, she may be maximizing the fulfillment of her (firm, consistent) present desires and preferences; but in that case, a preference-maximizing conception will have to treat her choice as perfectly or optimally rational, whereas, as we have seen, it is more commonsensical to regard such a choice as less than optimally rational if it expectably produces less good for the agent in the long run. And even if a preference-maximizing scheme somehow downgraded present impulse so that the maximization of value-weighted preferences required one to override such impulse in the name of long-term good, the result would simply be a variant on optimizing views and still leave no room for supererogation. Thus common-sense views about supererogatory extramoral rationality appear to be incompatible with optimizing, good-maximizing, and preference-maximizing views alike.

At this point we have completed our rough survey of common-sense rationality and its analogies with common-sense morality, and it is time for us to turn our main focus to the optimizing and maximizing models that have until now so totally eclipsed our ordinary thinking in this area. We shall see that these prevalent theories of rationality have some important problems and tasks of their own and, more particularly, that they cannot avoid spawning a whole host of competitors with underlying motivation similar to their own.

· 7 ·

Rationality-Consequentialism

In the *Methods of Ethics* Sidgwick examines what he takes to be the three main competing approaches to ethics: ethical egoism, utilitarianism, and common-sense intuitionism. Sidgwick does not strongly distinguish between the right and the rational—between moral and rational requirements—and so each of the "methods" is seen as offering a general view about what acts are both right and rational. One of the three methods, ethical egoism, is most naturally understood as developing out of a view of what is practically rational in the self-regarding sphere. An egoist, roughly, is someone who thinks an agent always ought to act in the way it is rational to act in circumstances where only the agent's self-interest or good is at stake. And since Sidgwick holds that one is rationally required to optimize (maximize) with respect to one's own good or happiness in situations where no other rational factors are relevant, it is natural for him to conceive egoism as the view that we are always morally and rationally required to do what is best for ourselves. (Sidgwick actually builds hedonism into his definition of egoism, but we can ignore this complication.)[1]

However, if the preceding chapters are on the right track, then Sidgwick miscounts the main possibilities for ethical theory. If the extramoral rational pursuit of one's own good need not be conceived in optimizing or maximizing terms, if a common-sense view of individualistic rationality like that outlined above is a distinct possibility, then there is a form of ethical egoism that corresponds to that view in just the way in which Sidgwick's conception of egoism generalizes, and corresponds to, the optimizing view of individualistic rationality. Sidgwick ignores this possibility because he somehow fails to recognize the existence of a distinctive common-sense view of what is rational. (Can this have been because of his tendency to run together the right and the rational?) But there is in fact a fourth "method of ethics," a form of egoism structurally more akin to common-sense morality than to optimizing utilitarianism, and its merits and demerits would need to be taken into account in any attempt to evaluate the methods Sidgwick does consider.

We are not, however, equating the right and the rational as Sidgwick did, and indeed our whole discussion of common-sense versus optimizing views reflects a widespread contemporary insistence on distinguishing these two concepts. Like Sidgwick, we are considering, or ought to be considering, four possible views or theories, but our manner of proceeding sharply segregates conceptions of morality from conceptions of rationality. We have not spoken of total views such as egoism except very tangentially: in speaking about what is rational we have restricted ourselves to extramoral contexts precisely because they do not raise the difficult issue of whether it is rational to be moral and do not force us to consider something that others have spent a great deal of time considering—but that lies apart, I believe, from our main enterprise—namely, totally general theories of what it is rational to do.

Yet what we have just been saying about such total theories should make it even clearer how very natural it is to pair optimizing consequentialism with an individually optimizing conception of practical rationality, and to oppose to them the pair consisting of common-sense morality and common-sense rationality. Indeed, all the analogies we have drawn between common-sense morality and common-sense rationality have taken optimizing morality and optimizing rationality as respective baselines, and the analogies would collapse if the latter were not already naturally and correctly seen as structurally similar. But let us review some of the reasons behind the similarity.

I

Standard consequentialism treats any act with overall better consequences as morally better than any alternative with less good consequences and demands the morally best act available to the agent. By the same token, an optimizing view of individualistic rationality insists on the universal rational preferability of choosing consequences that are better for oneself and requires the agent to choose the rationally best action available. By contrast with common-sense morality, impersonally judged good results are the only thing that counts morally for an act-consequentialist view, and in similar contrast with our picture of common-sense rationality, the optimizing model of individualistically rational choice treats the good of the agent as the only rational factor to be considered.

To be sure, this still leaves an important difference between standard consequentialism and the optimizing view of rational choice. The latter includes a relativity to the agent, whereas the former is entirely agent-neutral. But whatever the optimizing conception of rationality says about the agent's personal good, standard consequentialism says, or can say, about overall or impersonal good; and so *mutatis mutandis* they are almost exactly analogous. As a result, it can seem natural to think of the optimizing view of rational choice as a form of consequentialism, not about morality, but about rationality. But the difference in underlying relativity renders that assumption not strictly accurate. Consequentialism is almost always defined in terms of a concern for good impersonally judged, and a theory of rationality that requires the agent to seek what she has reason to believe will be best or most preference-satisfying *for her* is not in such terms a form of consequentialism.[2] I propose, then, to reserve the term "(act-)-consequentialism" for *moral* theories that evaluate solely in terms of impersonally judged good consequences, while at the same time using the label "rationality-consequentialism" to refer to any optimizing or maximizing view of individualistic, extramoral choice. The latter term focuses our attention on some highly important similarities, and it turns out, in addition, that we can no longer get by talking merely of optimizing or maximizing theories of rationality because the possibilities in this area are much richer than have yet been indicated.

We have already mentioned the possibility of satisficing forms of (utilitarian) act-consequentialism which can allow an act to count as right even if it has less good consequences than some available alternative. Such views are consequentialistic because they treat overall good consequences as the only thing relevant to act-evaluation and because, more particularly, they regard any act with overall consequences less good than those of some alternative as morally less good than that alternative. But they allow for supererogation and for the moral permissibility of less than optimal behavior. And there are precisely analogous possibilities open in the area of rational choice.

A theory of individual rationality can hold, for example, that good consequences for the agent are all that is rationally relevant, hold even that it is always rationally better for an agent to choose what is likely to have better results for herself, without being committed to the optimizing view's denial of rational supererogation. Even without bringing in our common-sense ideas about rational choice, there is conceptual space for a view that allows for less than optimal rational choice, that can treat certain choices as rational even though they have less good consequences for the agent, and are (thus) less rational, than certain available alternatives.

Similar points can be made if we understand extramoral rationality solely in terms of the satisfaction of extramoral preferences. A theory of rational choice can claim that the more rational choice is always the one whose consequences are or would be (expectably) more preference-satisfying for the agent, while at the same time allowing for rational supererogation in a way that the preference-maximizing view does not. It can admit, in other words, that a certain choice is less preference-satisfying and (so) *less rational* than some preference-maximizing alternative, but hold that the choice is nonetheless *rationally acceptable*. (For simplicity's sake I shall sometimes drop the reference to *extramoral* preferences.)

We therefore need a term for what the familiar optimizing and maximizing conceptions of extramoral rational choice have in common with other theories that judge the rationality of choices solely in terms of how good or preference-satisfying their consequences are for the agent, and I am proposing that we regard all such views as forms of *rationality-consequentialism*.[3] Whether we have any reason to prefer supererogation-permitting forms of rationality-consequentialism to the more familiar optimizing and maximizing forms is a topic we shall be taking up shortly. But armed with this new terminology and with the realization that there exist a number of possible views about rational choice running parallel to different forms of moral consequentialism, we need to consider another question first.

II

According to the traditional optimizing conception of individualistically rational choice, we ought (always) to aim at our own greatest happiness or greatest good.[4] And to a large extent either such a view or some preference-maximizing conception of rationality is standard in philosophy, economics, decision theory, and other disciplines concerned with individualistic practical rationality. But optimizing/maximizing views of rationality are stated in a wide variety of ways, so in speaking as I just have, I am obviously simplifying a quite complex picture. However, the important differences I am shunting aside do not bear on the important issues I would like to raise here; so I shall continue to speak in a simplifying manner in order to bring out some issues and distinctions that have been obscured or ignored in the vast literature where optimizing or maximizing is defended or taken for granted. The best way to bring out the issue that most immediately concerns us will be to turn to Sidgwick once again and consider his varying formulations of different and incompatible moral/rational conceptions.

Sidgwick sometimes characterizes the utilitarian (meaning, act–utilitarian) view of right and wrong in a manner strictly analogous to the way he formulates egoism. If the egoist thinks it is right and rational to aim at his own greatest happiness, then the utilitarian can be described as one who thinks it right and rational to aim at (the greatest) universal happiness, and Sidgwick makes it amply clear that he finds nothing particularly amiss in either characterization.[5] But in another place he gives utilitarianism an alternative formulation with very different moral implications. At the very beginning of his main discussion of utilitarianism Sidgwick says: "By Utilitarianism is here meant the ethical theory, that the conduct which, under any given circumstances, is objectively right, is that which will produce the greatest amount of happiness on the whole."[6]

Because Sidgwick gives this statement some prominence and has already said elsewhere[7] that his main concern will be with objective (as opposed to believed) rightness, the statement quoted has some claim, I think, to be considered Sidgwick's official formulation of the act–utilitarian view. And since Sidgwick almost immediately thereafter says that the view that universal happiness is the ultimate standard should not be taken to imply that universal benevolence is the only right or best motive of action, he would appear to hold that the rightness of actions does not, for a utilitarian, consist in aiming at the greatest general happiness, but rather in (somehow) doing that act which will actually lead to the greatest happiness. And in that case, all the talk about the rightness or rationality of aiming at universal happiness must be regarded as based on certain simplifying assumptions about the relation between motivation and justification.

There is nothing very puzzling about any of this: these distinctions are very much a part of current-day moral philosophy. What *is* puzzling is that Sidgwick offers no parallel distinctions in his discussion of egoism (or egoistic rationality). Egoism is characterized in terms of the agent's aiming for or seeking her own greatest good or happiness, and although the distinction between the standard of evaluation and the most desirable motivation emerges briefly at various points in the discussion, Sidgwick never claims that an act or choice is right in egoistic terms just in case, however motivated, it actually produces greater happiness for the agent than would any available alternative. Yet in practically every other way one can think of, Sidgwick stresses the analogies between egoism and utilitarianism; so it is somewhat surprising that the principle of egoism is never formulated in parallel with the most prominent statement of utilitarianism's greatest happiness principle. Sidgwick is usually so careful and thoroughgoing that it is difficult to accuse him of an oversight here, but on the other hand there seems to be no reason for him to formulate egoism and utilitarianism differently.

Yet formulating egoism in terms of actual consequences would entail some rather interesting results. Egoism, we have seen, is the generalization (and extension to the moral) of what one takes to be rational in extramoral cases where only the agent's good is at issue. So if there is no reason not to state egoism in actualistic terms, that is, in terms of the actual good for the agent produced by given choices or actions, then there would seem to be no reason not to state our principles of individualistic practical rationality in similar terms. Yet as far as I can tell, this is something philosophers never do. Maximizing or optimizing theorists of rational choice may say that a choice or act is rational if it has the greatest expectation value for the agent or if it is likely to produce the best results for the agent—or the agent is reasonable to think so—given the alternatives that are available. But I don't believe any philosopher has ever said that individualistically rational acts (choices) are those that actually lead to better or more preference-satisfying results for the agent than any alternative would have. And such views, of course, *conflict* with any attempt to characterize rationality in terms of likely or reasonably expected results.

Optimizing and maximizing theories of individual rationality are thus typically formulated in (what we can call) probabilistic, rather than actualist, terms, but I think we have good reason to wonder why this must inevitably be the case. Act-consequentialism is naturally seen as analogous to the principle of rational choice that applies to the single individual in extramoral circumstances,[8] and where there are competing formulations of (act-)consequentialism, it should be possible for there to be, *mutatis mutandis*, competing conceptions of individualistic rationality (and of rational egoism). Consequentialism is sometimes stated in probabilistic terms as holding that acts are right if they are (reasonably thought) likely to produce best (or tied-best) consequences; but sometimes it is put in actualist terms as claiming that acts are right if they in fact produce best consequences. Occasionally, indeed, the difference between these views is slurred—and the difficulty of deciding between them passed over—by saying that acts are right just in case they have or are likely to have best consequences. But the differing formulations and the attempts to smooth over differences between them both indicate the important place actualism about consequences has had in consequentialist thought. Why, then, has the possibility of a similar actualism about consequences-for-the-agent been neglected in the theory of rational choice?

Consequentialism (meaning, moral consequentialism) naturally comes in actualist and probabilistic varieties, and the currently predominant views of rational individualistic choice are, as we have seen, aptly characterized as forms of rationality-consequentialism. Isn't it time, then, to consider both actualistic and probabilistic formulations of the latter, despite the lack of historical precedents? (And isn't it time to consider actualist versions of egoism as well?)

Do not say at this point that the implications of actualistic optimizing or maximizing rationality-consequentialism are simply too implausible to be taken seriously. True, if we accept such a view, then an act can count as rational if through sheer luck or miscalculation it leads to better or more preference-fulfilling results for the agent than some alternative that was *likely* to have better or more preference-fulfilling results. This goes against common sense, to be sure. But actualistic optimizing/maximizing consequentialism also leads to intuitively strange results: it can turn out, as we have already seen, that it was wrong of Hitler's mother not to drown him in the bath when he was a baby, because of the actual, though unanticipatable results of her not doing so, and this goes against our common moral thinking in a very strange way.

Such counter-intuitiveness, however, has not deterred those consequentialists who give more credence to simplicity and explanatory power than to our ordinary sense of plausibility. And given the many parallels between act-consequentialism and rationality-consequentialism, and in particular their seemingly similar underlying motivations, one wonders why a defender of the latter could not or should

not invoke similar considerations in defending an actualistic version against the criticism of unintuitiveness. Probabilistic consequentialism and probabilistic rationality-
consequentialism have, of course, slightly less nonintuitive
implications than their actualist alternatives. But if intuitions
are to be taken seriously, one wonders why the consequentialist shouldn't give up even probabilistic consequentialism in
favor of common-sense morality, and why the rationality-
consequentialist shouldn't likewise retreat into the common-
sense view of rationality outlined in previous chapters.
Probabilistic versions of both consequentialism and rationality-consequentialism (and here the differences between the
familiar maximizing/optimizing forms and supererogation-
allowing versions are not at issue) are made more vulnerable if
one attempts to motivate them by citing their superior intuitiveness in comparison with their actualistic counterparts, and
that itself is a reason to take such counterparts seriously.

Actualistic moral consequentialism, of course, has been and
currently is taken very seriously both by critics and by defenders of consequentialism. Some of this serious consideration is
based on the previously noted capacity (or partial capacity) of
actualistic consequentialism to make irenic concessions to
common-sense plausibility: even if Hitler's mother is said to
act wrongly, it can also be said that she is not blameworthy for
what she did, since blaming her would not produce (would
not have produced) good or optimal results. But actualistic
rationality-consequentialism can be given a similar boost by
pointing out that an act with unexpectedly bad results, which
thereby counts as irrational, may still not count as rationally
(or morally) criticizable if acts of criticizing it would do little
or no good (for their agents).

Moreover, in recent years the tendency has actually been to
prefer actualistic versions of (utilitarian) act-consequentialism
over their probabilistic counterparts. This has come about in
some measure through increasing self-consciousness about

the underlying rational psychology of utilitarianism and, more particularly, through a tendency to view moral judgment as most properly made from a standpoint of impersonal (or impartial or rational) benevolence subject to none of the usual limitations of human knowledge.[9] According to utilitarianism or consequentialism thus understood, moral judgment is ideally to be made *sub specie aeternitatis*, from a viewpoint freed from identity with any particular time, place, or person. Since limitations in our knowledge result from particularities of time, place, and person, but are transcended in a *sub specie aeternitatis* view of things, a consequentialism grounded in this way will regard all facts as relevant to valid moral judgments. An act which (from the point of view of its agent and others with similar limitations) has unexpectedly good overall long-run results will then be treated as morally right because it would have been favored or approved by an all-knowing impersonally benevolent being aware of all its consequences. And there will be no reason to tie the rightness or obligatoriness of acts to what is likely or reasonably believed from the limited standpoint of actual agents.

But if—*if*—one holds that an all-knowing benevolent standpoint is the proper fulcrum for valid moral judgment, why should not the same hold true for assessments of rational choice and action? Some consequentialists have regarded their attempt to free the making of moral judgments from all limitations of perspective as a way of making moral judgment more rational (hence all the talk of "rational benevolence"). But if such moves toward greater rationality are justified in moral theory, surely they are all the more justified *in the theory of rationality itself.* Anyone who prefers actualistic versions of consequentialism—and this will include many critics as well as defenders of act-consequentialism—would seem to have reason to hold that any judgment about the individualistic rationality of a given act or choice is most correctly or properly made from an all-knowing standpoint of benevolence (exclusively) toward its agent. So a commitment to the preferability of actualistic over probabilistic versions of consequentialism will entail a similar preference between versions of rationality-consequentialism, and at the very least, given what appears to be a total absence of philosophically convincing reasons for preferring probabilistic over actualistic rationality-consequentialism, we must certainly take the latter seriously. Although it has long been ignored by philosophers and others, it represents a serious alternative in the theory of individualistic rational choice.[10] But having ourselves during the present section ignored the distinction between supererogation-denying and supererogation-allowing forms of rationality-consequentialism, it is time to turn again to that topic. Let us drop the question of actualism versus probabilism and simply assume that any version of rationality-consequentialism can come in either actualistic or probabilistic form. However, relative to that assumption, we still need to consider whether rationality-consequentialism is best formulated in an optimizing or maximizing version that leaves no room for rational supererogation, or whether one or another supererogation-permitting conception of rationality-consequentialism may not be theoretically preferable.

III

Unlike the common-sense rationality detailed in previous chapters, rationality-consequentialism treats (expectable) good or preference-fulfilling consequences for the agent as the only thing relevant to the rationality of acts and choices (and of habits of decision-making and dispositions to choose as well, but we shall concentrate mainly on the application of rationality-consequentialism, and of common-sense views, to single acts or choices). Rationality-consequentialism therefore treats a choice or act as less rational than some alternative if—roughly speaking—it will (probably) have less good or less preference-satisfying long-term consequences for the agent, but by itself this thesis does not entail that the former choice or act is simply irrational. Traditional, standard optimizing views of extramoral rationality assent to the further claim that it is extramorally irrational to do anything that will probably have less than optimal results for oneself, thus denying the possibility of rational supererogation. But we have pointed out that another view is conceivable according to which (expectably) better consequences for the agent make for greater rationality, but the (expectable) achievement of best consequences for the agent is not a condition of rationality *simpliciter*. And we have seen that similar possibilities exist when extramoral rationality is understood in terms of the (expectable) satisfaction of extramoral preferences.

To put the matter somewhat roughly, such views say that there is some level of resultant preference satisfaction or good consequences for the agent less than the most/best achievable which it can be rational enough for an agent to seek or achieve. That level, though less than the most/best (likely to be) achievable, is sufficiently preference-satisfying or good for the agent that it needn't be treated as simply irrational for the agent to achieve or aim for it. Given the obvious parallelism with the forms of satisficing moral consequentialism discussed briefly in Chapter 1, we can designate views of this kind as forms of satisficing rationality-consequentialism; and the optimizing and maximizing conceptions of practical rationality can then be referred to as optimizing and maximizing rationality-consequentialism. (But do not confuse satisficing rationality-consequentialism with the idea of rational satisficing. From the standpoint of a moderate individual, it can be more rational to satisfice than to optimize; whereas rationality-consequentialism always regards it as *less* rational to satisfice, but at the same time allows that such less than optimal rationality is sometimes not irrational.)

The idea of satisficing rationality-consequentialism, though of course it bears important relations to the economists' notion of satisficing, is not in itself a familiar notion. But its coherence is not, I think, to be doubted, and we should therefore consider what merits it has or lacks in comparison with the most familiar optimizing and maximizing forms of rationality-consequentialism.

We saw earlier that optimizing and maximizing views of rationality allow for infinitistic cases of rational dilemma; and it should be clear that good-satisficing or preference-satisficing rationality-consequentialism might evade such dilemmas by making the right sort of accommodations to rational supererogation. What is not clear, however, is that the ability to evade certain rational dilemmas is any sort of merit from the general standpoint of rationality-consequentialism. If rationality-consequentialism is to be understood and defended in the manner of moral act-consequentialism, then the intuitive repugnance of the idea of rational dilemma will count, in its terms, for very little. As I mentioned in Chapter 5, there appears to be little reason, from a standpoint not essentially tied to common-sense intuition, to seek to evade the possibility of rational dilemmas, and so the ability of satisficing rationality-consequentialism to avoid infinitistic or other dilemmas does not, in its own terms, count as an advantage over its optimizing/maximizing alternatives.

These alternatives may be felt to have an advantage because of the vagueness of the notion of good enough—or sufficiently preference-satisfying—consequences. But even if an unelaborated notion of the good enough or the sufficient is merely a placeholder for further specification, the notion of optimal—or maximally satisfying—consequences (for the agent) is also vague enough to call for a good deal of elaboration, and since no one has yet offered any very elaborate or formally precise account of the morally or the rationally "good enough," we should at this point perhaps be asking whether there is any reason to believe that a worked-out version of satisficing rationality-consequentialism would inevitably pall by comparison with the fairly specific maximizing or optimizing theories of rational choice that are by now familiar. (Perhaps methodological conservatism could allow us not to consider this question or to bother working out one or another form of satisficing rationality-consequentialism, but at this point I don't think we need or would want, most of us, to be *that* conservative.)

Can we say, for example, that it is less arbitrary to treat the choice with best, or most preference-fulfilling, results for the agent as the only rational choice than to specify one of the almost infinitely many levels less than the best or most as sufficiently rational? (I ignore for the moment the likelihood that what counts as enough will vary from situation to situation.) I think it is just as arbitrary to insist on the best or most and turn down all the lesser levels, and it hardly seems more arbitrary, for example, to pick out some halfway mark and designate choices as rational when and only when their consequences for the agent are at least half as good—or preference-satisfying—as what the agent could have achieved (or are above the average or median amount of personal good—or preference-satisfaction—achievable by the agent, relative to the set of his alternatives).

Aside from questions of arbitrariness, the issue of simplicity and explanatory power matters as well. In the literature of economics, this has long been thought to raise problems for satisficing views and to represent an advantage for maximizing/optimizing accounts of rational choice. But if we look at the matter from a more abstract or philosophical perspective, it is again not clear that the advantage, in terms of simplicity or explanatory power, must inevitably lie with the latter. It is not clear, to begin with, that the halfway views mentioned just above are substantially less simple than optimizing/maximizing conceptions. (Consider too the earlier mentioned, even simpler satisficing view, which treats an act as rational whenever it has good consequences on balance for the agent.) And the issue of explanatory power may in fact very much depend on issues about the prevalence of human practical irrationality that are nowadays hotly debated and seem far from any definitive resolution.

Halfway versions of satisficing rationality-consequentialism are presumably too simple, or simple-minded, to be taken seriously as alternatives to an elaborated optimizing theory. So plausible worked-out versions of satisficing rationality-consequentialism may need to base their account of enoughness, not on purely formal or mathematical considerations, but on some account of the relations between practical activity and human flourishing and/or desire. What counts as good enough or sufficiently fulfilling for the agent may relate to basic human satisfactions and general human needs (consider that Popper's negative utilitarianism emphasizes the elimination of unsatisfactory situations over the promotion of bliss or intense happiness).[11] But it will also presumably have something to do with how well our practical rational capacities are "designed" for the production of the things we need and want in the ordinary circumstances of human life. These and a host of related issues will have to be taken up by someone seeking to formulate a specific, but simple and explanatorily rich account of rationality that allows for rational satisficing but is strictly rationality-consequentialist. But it is perhaps also worth again mentioning the intuitive plausibility, the common-sense acceptability, of allowing for rational supererogation.

Although it is widely assumed that a maximizing or optimizing conception of extramoral rationality best accounts for our ordinary practice and intuitions, we have seen how natural it is to describe certain cases of rational choice in terms that allow for rational supererogation. Satisficing rationality-consequentialism does allow for rational supererogation and is to that extent, I believe, more in line with ordinary thinking.

And although this better fit with common sense may not be much of an advantage from the standpoint of approaches to rationality and morality that give common sense and intuition little credence, still, from the standpoint of those not committed to such a wholesale rejection of common sense, the ability to accommodate rational supererogation may seem a major virtue of satisficing rationality-consequentialism.

However, it is also worth noting that some of the ways in which common sense makes room for rational supererogation are very different from anything allowable within a rationality-consequentialist framework. The time-relative permissions of common-sense rationality allow a greater emphasis on present or near-future goods and desires. Someone who achieves less overall good for himself by giving in to some impulse of the present need not count as acting irrationally, and resistance to such an impulse may thus be considered rationally supererogatory from an ordinary standpoint. Now satisficing rationality-consequentialism may also allow for the rationality of giving in to an impulse of the sort just mentioned, but it cannot justify such a claim by invoking a rational permission to favor nearer over more distant times; any such theory must be neutral regarding future times (as indeed any form of moral consequentialism will also be), and—if it focuses on personal good rather than on preference-satisfaction—its justification for allowing less than personally optimific action on impulse will in fact have to depend on whether such action produces *enough* good (over time) for the agent. The possibilities such satisficing rationality-consequentialism provides for rational supererogation will also therefore have to depend on factors of this sort and be independent of the above-mentioned form of temporal relativity.

By the same token, a satisficing rationality-consequentialism that focuses on personal good may be able to treat some of the examples of intrinsic moderation described in earlier chapters as rational, but will have different reasons from those invoked by the common-sense advocate of moderation. The latter may regard herself as sometimes having more reason to satisfice than to optimize. Taking or asking for more good than she needs may in her terms be less rational than taking or asking for something less good for herself; it may even be simply irrational. But a rationality-consequentialist who thinks in terms of the promotion of human good will have to regard such moderation as less rational than optimizing and can avoid treating it as irrational only by holding that the moderate agent does well enough for herself so that she shouldn't be regarded as acting simply irrationally. On the other hand, as we saw in Chapter 1, a preference-maximizing form of rationality-consequentialism can treat non-instrumental moderation as optimally rational, and the same, of course, will be true of any preference-oriented version of satisficing rationality-consequentialism.

IV

At this point, advocates of optimizing or maximizing rationality may feel tempted to invoke the foundational psychology of utilitarian consequentialism in an effort to show the superiority of optimizing or maximizing to satisficing forms of rationality-consequentialism. We have already seen that consequentialism sometimes calls upon the notion of (all-knowing) impersonal benevolence in grounding its principle(s) of right action, and that rationality-consequentialism can appeal to a notion of (all-knowing) benevolence toward an agent in grounding its notion(s) of what it is rational for a particular agent to do. And it may be felt that such conceptions of morality and rationality will tend to yield optimizing as opposed to satisficing theories.

From the standpoint of utilitarian, consequentialist morality, for example, it seems natural to conceive right actions as those that would be approved or found acceptable by an all-knowing, or at least relevantly informed, being who was impersonally or impartially concerned with the well-being/happiness of all. But is it clear that such a conception would favor optimizing over satisficing forms of act-consequentialism? Why should such an impersonally benevolent being approve only those acts with optimal consequences? Granting that such a being will favor or prefer acts with optimal consequences over alternatives with less good overall consequences, does it follow that such a being will find those alternatives—even those with *very good* consequences—unacceptable, unworthy of her approbation? Perhaps the benevolent onlooker will be pleased by acts producing less-than-optimal good consequences, even though certain optimific alternatives would have pleased her *more*. (Indeed, it is not even clear that someone with the *highest degree* of benevolence would have to *disapprove* of what she found less than ideal in the production of human happiness or well-being.)

Part of the intuitive force of act-utilitarianism lies in its use of the notion of benevolence, together with rational constraints like impersonality and, in some versions, omniscience, to deliver its consequentialist view of morality. And it has certainly been assumed by Sidgwick and others that these conditions uniquely determine an optimizing/maximizing standard of right and wrong. But the foundational moral psychology of act-utilitarianism (and, it could be shown, of act-consequentialism more generally) in fact allows a modeling of all those common-sense considerations favoring the idea of moral supererogation—and so it seems to have no way to rule out satisficing forms of moral consequentialism.

By the same token, nothing in the earlier suggested foundations for rationality-consequentialism entails a preference for optimizing/maximizing over satisficing versions. If extramoral rationality is to be judged from the perspective of an individual—all-knowing or not—who is completely and exclusively concerned with the well-being or good of a given agent, how can we say that such an individual would not find certain acts with very good but less-than-optimal consequences for the agent both acceptable and pleasing? I conclude, then, that both optimizing/maximizing act-consequentialism and optimizing/maximizing rationality-consequentialism are underdetermined by the foundational considerations it is natural to bring forward in their behalf. And there are additional reasons for this conclusion.

Imagine, for example, the situation of someone who cannot help harming people. This person has contracted a particularly virulent form of plague, and wherever she goes (and even if she stays put) she will infect people—different people depending on what she does—via various carriers of the disease. Is any series of actions performable by such an agent likely to be acceptable to or elicit the approval of a totally and impersonally benevolent being?[12] We saw earlier that it is possible to be morally unhappy with, or rationally rueful of, situationally best actions with terrible consequences, so the fact that an act has better or more preference-fulfilling consequences (for the agent) than its alternatives may not suffice to elicit approval or acceptance from the appropriate benevolent observer. Once again, the usual foundational psychology seems inadequate to ground standard optimizing and maximizing views, and as a result we may need to add further conditions to such views or else reformulate their foundational psychology.[13]

But there is another possibility. The underdetermination we have considered can certainly be viewed as calling for better consequentialist or rationality-consequentialist theories of what is right and what is rational. But at this point, we may attempt to outflank the problems of underdetermination by means of a new kind of theory, a new approach, in this area. All the consequentialist views of morality we have been considering have a common structure, and perhaps the truth about consequentialist morality and invulnerability to the difficulties mentioned above are confined to the common part. And it may be possible to make the same point with regard to rationality-consequentialism as well.

We have already given some indication of what is common to all act-consequentialist moral views. Such views may differ as to how much good to require for right action, but all agree in treating any act as morally better than some alternative if and only if it has better overall consequences than that alternative. (Even a view which treats certain choices among evils as allowing of no right action can treat the action with best consequences as better than its alternatives.) Of course, I am bracketing the issue of actualism versus probabilism, but putting that question momentarily aside, it should be clear that both satisficing and optimizing forms of consequentialism treat the goodness of consequences as the only thing relevant to moral evaluation, thereby agreeing in their comparative moral judgments even while differing in positive assessments. The various consequentialist views we are considering thus differ only in where they draw the line between right and wrong, and this leaves a vast area of agreement on comparative judgments that may be used to form the basis of a moral view that *restricts itself* to comparative moral judgments. Scalar act-consequentialism, as it is appropriate to call it, would provide for all the comparative moral assessments common to differing forms of act-consequentialism while explicitly excluding the positive judgments of right and wrong that give rise to their differences. I have described such a theory elsewhere at some length,[14] but its main features can be indicated as follows.

Differences between optimizing and satisficing consequentialism, or between different versions of satisficing (or optimizing) consequentialism, as to where to draw the line between right and wrong may be no more resolvable in objective or rational terms than differences about where to draw the line between baldness and non-baldness. In that case, any consequentialist ethics that seeks an objective account of morality will do best explicitly to exclude the making of judgments of right and wrong and to confine itself to comparative judgments of morally better and worse. One could then preserve and make use of the traditional foundational psychology of (all-knowing) impersonal benevolence by focusing on the preferences or other *comparative attitudes* of an impersonally benevolent (omniscient) being. Whether or not such a being would be displeased by an optimal act with bad consequences, she would clearly prefer or favor such an act over an alternative with even worse consequences; and whether or not an act with "good enough" consequences would be approved by such a being, presumably an alternative with even better consequences would be even more pleasing to her. So one can preserve a version of moral consequentialism and its underlying psychology on a purely scalar basis (we have been speaking in actualist terms just to simplify the points being made); but such a theory clearly leaves out questions and answers which previous consequentialism has felt the need to insist upon. Without making judgments of right and wrong, a moral view may seem insufficiently action-guiding or practical and may seem incapable of giving us a complete account of morality.

But act-consequentialism is in a particularly poor position to insist that correct moral theories be capable of a useful action-guiding role. The history of utilitarianism is strewn with disclaimers, in behalf of the principle of utility, of any reason to expect it to function as a practical moral guide. And it would be difficult for consequentialists to point to limitations in the action-guiding capacities of scalar consequentialism as any argument against the fundamental correctness of such a restricted view. Certainly, scalar consequentialism *may* not tell the whole (consequentialist) story. Future developments may show us how to defend some particular form of satisficing or optimizing act-consequentialism against all comers, allowing us in some one particular way to make the sorts of positive moral judgments consequentialists and others have always wanted to make. But if now, or at some later date, we feel that the variety of views in this area and their underdetermination relative to traditional foundations indicate the absence of any objectively correct consequentialist view of right and wrong, rather than provide a reason for pressing on with better arguments and evidence for some particular consequentialist view of right and wrong, then scalar act-consequentialism may well turn out to encapsulate the more limited moral truth that consequentialism is capable of uncovering.

Now of course the above considerations have been focused on consequentialist moral theories. But it should be clear, *mutatis mutandis*, that they can likewise be directed toward rationality-consequentialism. Both satisficing and optimizing/maximizing rationality-consequentialism (and even those forms of the latter that insist on *more* than optimization or maximization, that is, on minimally *good* or *satisfaction-increasing* results for the agent, as a condition of rational choice) are underdetermined from a standpoint of all-knowing, or even just appropriately informed, benevolence toward the agent. But a scalar form of rationality-consequentialism may outflank this difficulty by confining itself to comparative judgments about which alternative acts it would be more or less rational for an agent to perform and by insisting that no further truth is to be had in this area, no non-arbitrary way of drawing the line between rational and irrational choices within realistic sets of alternatives. All rationality-consequentialist views rank alternatives in terms of the (probable) goodness or satisfyingness of their consequences, and such a comparative ranking is sustained rather than brought into question by invoking a standpoint of informed or all-knowing benevolence toward the agent. Whether such benevolence will approve or disapprove an optimal act that does much harm to the agent or a less-than-optimal act that does much good, it clearly will *prefer* an agent-harmful act to its even more harmful alternatives and be *less willing to accept* a non-optimally agent-beneficial act than some alternative more beneficial to the agent. (The same points can be made regarding preference-satisfaction.) And these clear-cut results may then be taken as the only ones we have a right to rely on in attempting to formulate a theoretically objective rationality-consequentialist view. The sole truth about rational choice and action might thus turn out to be encapsulable within a scalar view that limits itself to comparative judgments and deliberately excludes drawing the line between what is rational and what is irrational.[15]

Of course, one may reply at this point that such a view subverts the original intention theories of rationality have of providing criteria for making positive attributions of rationality and irrationality (and for guiding actions). And there may be some reason to believe, or hope, that we may eventually be able to show the superiority of some particular form of optimizing, maximizing, or satisficing rationality-consequentialism over competing views of what is and is not rational. But failing such an outcome, a scalar view of rational choice —or, rather, of *more or less* rational choice—may be the best and most objective theory achievable from a rationality-consequentialist perspective, and, as with act-consequentialism, we may have to abandon some of our original hopes and aims if we are in this area to achieve the theoretical objectivity we have also been seeking.

The scalar theory we would then be left with may in fact have application beyond the sphere of acts and choices. We have been understanding rationality-consequentialism as applying to particular acts or choices, and so understood, a scalar version holds that possible acts or choices are more rational than alternatives if and only if they have (or are likely to have) better—or more preference-satisfying—consequences for their agents than those alternatives. But it is also possible to be a rationality-consequentialist about habits of decision-making, and on a scalar view one such possible habit counts as rationally superior or preferable to some alternative habit if and only if its consequences for the agent (or for agents generally, depending on how narrowly we individuate habits and on some related issues) are better—more preference-fulfilling—than those of the alternative. As with particular actions, a scalar view would have to preclude the possibility of objectively correct positive judgments about the rationality or irrationality of habits, and it seems likely that if one goes scalar with the evaluation of acts and choices, one will wish to do so with habits of choice and other objects of rationality-evaluation. So in the end I think it is possible for a rationality-consequentialist to advocate an across-the-board scalar view for reasons quite similar to those which may move the moral consequentialist toward the scalar.

Once one recognizes the *possibility* of satisficing act-consequentialism, the question where to draw the line between consequences good enough for rightness and consequences not good enough may seem incapable of objective, non-arbitrary solution, and scalar act-consequentialism appears as a theoretical option with much to recommend it. The possibility of pushing on with consequentialist attempts to draw the line between right and wrong is hardly excluded, and may well, for many, remain the preferred alternative, but the idea that we should explicitly restrict ourselves to comparative judgments has, I think, some considerable attractions in our present circumstances. And much the same can be said in favor of scalar rationality-consequentialism regarding acts, choices, or other objects of rational assessment. The analogies between standard moral consequentialism and the received optimizing view of rationality originally led us to speak of the latter—and then, by extension, of the preference-maximizing view as well—as a form of rationality-consequentialism. But those same analogies lead us to consider optimizing/maximizing and satisficing versions both of moral act-consequentialism and of rationality-consequentialism, and this, in turn, gives us some impetus toward a purely scalar view both of morality and of rationality.

We have seen that the currently dominant optimizing and maximizing views of rational choice are only a limited sample of a whole host of rationality-consequentialist theories. Some of these theories compete with the dominant views by virtue of their judgments about what is rational and irrational; the scalar conception competes, however, in a much deeper way by denying the possibility of judging rationality or irrationality *simpliciter*. And it is still very unclear from which of these two directions the greater challenge to current views is likely to emerge.

· 8 ·

Implications for Ethics

Prevalent theories of rational choice, as we have seen, are open
to challenge from within their own intellectual traditions.
Both optimizing and maximizing views are naturally and
properly described as forms of rationality-consequentialism.
But the same considerations that allow act-consequentialism
to be formulated in actualist fashion suggest that neither the
optimizing nor the preference-maximizing view of individual
rationality is necessarily best conceived in the probabilistic
terms in which it is normally stated. Moreover, attempts to
ground rationality-consequentialism in the notion of benevolence toward an agent do not clearly distinguish between
optimizing or maximizing views and a number of clear-cut
alternatives.

Thus there are satisficing forms of rationality-consequentialism (still to be worked out) which deny the universal necessity of optimizing or maximizing, and supplemented forms of
rationality-consequentialism which treat optimizing or maximizing as sometimes insufficient for rational choice, and theories of both kinds seem as compatible with the foundational
motivations of rationality-consequentialism as the maximizing or optimizing views are. And if it turns out—as at present
we have some reason to fear—that the latter are in this way
underdetermined by the best considerations that can be put
forward in their favor, it may also be reasonable to abandon all

views judging of positive rationality or irrationality and accept
a scalar rationality-consequentialism that makes only comparative judgments.

All these reasons for doubting or denying the currently
dominant views are, as I said, generated from their own
natural roots and underlying justifications. In earlier discussions, we also saw the error in the widespread assumption that
some sort of optimizing or maximizing view is our common
everyday standard of individualistic practical rationality.
There is a common-sense view, or amalgam of views, concerning what it is rational or irrational to choose, but it diverges widely from any maximizing/optimizing view and
from every other form of rationality-consequentialism. Unlike the various forms of rationality-consequentialism, the
common-sense view is based in and supported by intuitive
considerations, and in that respect and with respect to its main
features common-sense rationality is analogous to common-
sense morality.

In moral theory, intuitiveness is a much disputed desideratum and the appeal to intuitions a much disputed form of
theoretical argument. But the same can be said for theoretical
simplicity, unity, and explanatory power. Defenders of common-sense views (and many of these would oppose talk of a
common-sense "theory" of right and wrong) question the
need for and force of considerations of simplicity, and so on,
within the sphere of the moral; but by the same token defenders of optimizing act-consequentialism question the usefulness
of intuitions and attack common-sense morality for its complexity and disunity.

Until now, however, no such disagreement has occurred in
the theory of rational choice: the optimizing view—or some
maximizing version thereof—has been tacitly regarded as
combining the theoretical power of moral consequentialism
with the intuitive roots of common-sense morality. And a
major aim of the present book has been to show that such a

combination of virtues cannot be found within the sphere of individual rational choice. The previous chapters have attempted to demonstrate by argument and example that rational choice theory must be split into opposing views whose opposition is largely analogous with that between ordinary morality and (optimizing) act-consequentialism. Those who rely on intuition in deciding about the correctness of moral views will therefore have reason, in all consistency, to question preference-maximizing or good-optimizing views—or any other rationality-consequentialist theory of extramoral rational choice—and to favor the more intuitive standards we outlined in earlier chapters. So what we have said in these pages may weaken the hold of currently dominant views in two distinct ways: by showing us their underdetermination relative to the considerations that can be or are usually brought forward in their behalf; and by pointing out the existence of a totally different conception of self-regarding rational choice that embodies our intuitions in a way that no optimizing or maximizing view is capable of doing.

I don't want to spend time here—a vast literature would have to be critically examined—deciding on the respective merits, within ethical theory, of appeals to common intuition and to theoretical simplicity and unifying power. But what I have said on these topics should at least indicate that it is as appropriate and necessary to debate the relative merits of the optimizing/maximizing view of rationality (or of rationality-consequentialism) and of common-sense rationality as it is and has been to debate the relative merits of optimizing consequentialism and common-sense morality. And since we are presumably interested not only in having correct views about rational choice and right action taken separately, but also in having a correct total ethical view of rationality-cum-morality, we must also consider the effect of what we have been saying on ethical views in this larger sense.

Clearly, if we are going to combine ideas about morality

with ideas about extramoral rationality, it makes sense to combine common-sense rationality with common-sense morality and to combine rationality-consequentialism with act-consequentialism in the usual sense. The former combination will allow of a satisfying, an intellectually satisfying, symmetry between its moral and its rational parts, but it will be a symmetry between what we have seen to be highly complex views, and so common-sense rationality-cum-morality will on the whole be more complex than any alternative that combines a form of moral consequentialism with a form—presumably, an analogous form—of rationality-consequentialism. On the other hand, an optimizing, maximizing, satisficing, or scalar theory in the latter mold will compound the divergences from intuition that are to be found in rationality-consequentialism and in consequentialism taken separately, so those for whom intuitive plausibility is a touchstone of adequacy in ethics are likely to find a theory combining consequentialism with rationality-consequentialism more repugnant than either one of these considered in isolation.[1] Considering theories of rationality and of morality together does not solve our problems in ethics, but at the very least I think it helps us to see more clearly where the lines of division and disagreement actually lie. And it also makes a difference to the case for or against particular moral conceptions.

For example, there is a long tradition in ethics of seeking to draw analogies between individualistic rationality and morality and, more particularly, of basing moral views or theories in conceptions of practical rationality. Thus act-utilitarianism is often seen as basing itself on a natural conception of individualistic rationality: if that involves the maximization of the agent's well-being or satisfactions, then morality, which concerns all mankind, can be understood analogously as requiring the maximization of the well-being or satisfactions of everyone affected by a given act. And it is widely considered an advantage of act-utilitarianism that it facilitates such a symmetrical, and to that extent simple and unified, conception of morality-cum-rationality.

That is not to say that such analogies cannot be criticized. Rawls notably regards the act-utilitarian attempt to analogize between rational and moral choice as based on a misguided view of the nature of individuals, on a failure to recognize the separateness of individuals; but even Rawls accepts the utilitarians' optimizing/maximizing view of rational self-regarding choice and recognizes the prima facie attractiveness of basing a conception of morality on an analogy with the correct theory of individualistic rational choice.[2] Since Rawls's argument that the act-utilitarian analogy is based on a faulty metaphysics has itself turned out to be highly problematic,[3] there is certainly still life in the utilitarian or consequentialist idea of basing moral theory in an analogy with the theory of rational choice, and since, moreover, both consequentialists and anti-consequentialists have tended to accept an optimizing rationality-consequentialist conception of self-regarding rationality, optimizing (utilitarian) consequentialism has retained some powerful motivations.

However, once we recognize the possibility that even self-regarding rationality need not be conceived as optimizing or maximizing or as tied only to the production of good (or preference-satisfying) consequences for the agent, a powerful prop of optimizing or maximizing moral consequentialism is removed. For then, even if one wishes to take advantage of analogies between rational choice and morality, rationality will no longer be seen as having to assume a rationality-consequentialist or optimizing/maximizing form. And insistence on the analogy with individual rationality will not necessarily prevent moral theory from moving toward satisficing act-consequentialism, or toward scalar act-consequentialism, or toward common-sense morality.

More particularly, the case we have made for the existence of a common-sense understanding of rational choice helps to support the common-sense morality against a number of possible objections based on the force of the analogy between the moral and the individually rational. For example, the optimizing view of rationality requires optimization of the agent's good as a condition of rationality; but to the extent that common-sense rationality permits one to do less than the best for oneself, the common-sense moral view that one is not obligated to do the best one can for all mankind can be maintained compatibly with the desire to think of rationality and morality in parallel terms. While we thought that rationality could only be conceived in optimizing or maximizing fashion, common-sense morality's permission of less-than-maximal beneficence seemed out of keeping with the requirements of rationality, but our discussion of satisficing removes this barrier at least to common-sense morality by allowing the defender of common sense to hold a satisficing view both of morality and of rationality.

Common-sense morality has also seemed suspect for imposing limitations on impersonal optimizing and maximizing having no parallel in the optimizing or maximizing view of individual rationality. Yet again, once one sees that common-sense rationality contains restrictions on individual optimizing and maximizing, act-consequentialism no longer appears to be the inevitable choice for someone who takes the analogy between morality and rationality seriously, and common-sense deontology is correspondingly strengthened.

Now we have seen that the moderate, satisficing individual need not regard his choices and actions as less rational than their optimizing alternatives. From such a standpoint, the balance of reasons can favor the satisficing choice and that choice will therefore not count as less than ideally or optimally rational. So the idea of rational satisficing does not automatically entail the possibility of rational supererogation. Relative to the discussion in Chapter 1, then, the idea that individualistic rational choice allows no possibility of rational

supererogation remains intact, and so a second prop of optimizing (utilitarian) act-consequentialism remains in place.
For if rationality does not allow of supererogation (and of less-
than-optimal exemplification), then the desire for analogy
between morality and rationality will force us to criticize
common-sense morality and satisficing moral consequentialism for their commitment to the possibility of *moral*
supererogation.

Of course we might not insist on the fullest sort of analogy
between morality and rationality and might take the possibility of rational satisficing as in itself a good reason to allow for
moral satisficing, for morally permissible but less than maximally beneficent actions with morally supererogatory alternatives. This could lead either to some form of satisficing act-
consequentialism or to common-sense morality itself,
without forcing us to accept the possibility of *rational*
supererogation. However, we have seen independent reasons
for allowing rational supererogation as a theoretical alternative, and this, then, removes another prop of traditional
supererogation-denying act-consequentialism. If rational supererogation is no longer precluded, then moral supererogation is given new life either in a satisficing-consequentialist or
common-sense incarnation.

Thinking, then, in terms of total views of rationality-cum-
morality while at the same time insisting on substantial analogy between the two parts of any plausible total view, we have
at least the following possibilities: an optimizing/maximizing
view both of morality and of rationality; satisficing views of
both; scalar views of both; and a common-sense view of
morality and rationality. Of these four, only the last calls for
restrictions on permissible (personal or impersonal) optimiz-
ing/maximizing. And it is fairly clear in the light of recent
work that the deontological restrictions of common-sense
morality are the most controversial and problematic respect in
which such morality diverges from standard optimizing or

maximizing act-consequentialism; furthermore, Chapters 3 and 4 demonstrate the problematic character of common-sense *rational* restrictions. However, our ability to point to common-sense rational restrictions may do something for the cause of common-sense deontology, and for a common-sense view of both rationality and morality, by making such deontology seem less idiosyncratic than it otherwise might. (But that aspect of common-sense deontology which we earlier saw to lack any clear rational analogue will continue to seem quirky and dubious.)

However, as I mentioned before, all these adjustments in the support available to common-sense morality do not decide the issue of its validity. The burden of proof may shift, certain strong objections may be dissolved, but one is still left (at least) with the total views we have been at such pains to describe, and no argument or evidence available to us at present is capable, I think, of settling the issue among them. Nevertheless, quite apart from questions of validity, it is important to see how much wider our options are than has usually been recognized. We have turned up a surprising number of theories—both rational and moral—in the broadly utilitarian tradition, and as I have pointed out from the start, the existence of a distinctive common-sense form of practical rationality has long gone unnoticed. Even if we eventually prefer some form of rationality-consequentialism, our attempt here to describe some of the contours of common-sense rationality will have been worth it if it helps us to a better understanding of ourselves and our lives.

If the present book is on the right track, then ethics—leaving aside questions about Kantianism and virtue ethics—is in a highly unsettled condition. Clearly, a great deal of work will be needed before we can attain clarity and confidence about foundational issues. Nevertheless, I think there is every good reason to undertake that work and, in the light of the progress that has been made in recent years, to hope for further progress in the future.

Notes
Index

Notes

1. Moderation and Satisficing

1. See Henry Sidgwick, *The Methods of Ethics* (London: Macmillan, 1907), 7th ed., pp. 119–122, 381–382, 497–509; and John Rawls, *A Theory of Justice* (Cambridge: Harvard University Press, 1971), pp. 23–27, 416–424.

2. See Amartya Sen's "Utilitarianism and Welfarism," *Journal of Philosophy* 76 (1979), 470–471; and Charles Fried's *An Anatomy of Values* (Cambridge: Harvard University Press, 1970), pp. 170–176.

3. For relevant discussions in the economics literature of satisficing, see, for instance, Herbert Simon, "A Behavioral Model of Rational Choice," *Quarterly Journal of Economics* 69 (1955), 99–118; Simon, "Theories of Decision Making in Economics and Behavioral Science," *American Economic Review* 49 (1959), 253–283; Simon, *Administrative Behavior* (New York: Macmillan, 1961), 2nd ed.; and R. Cyert and J. March, eds., *A Behavioral Theory of the Firm* (Englewood Cliffs: Prentice-Hall, 1963).

4. *Rational* satisficing seems to require not only a disinclination to optimize, but a reasonable sense of when one has enough. To be content with much less than one should be is (can be) one form of *bathos*. Moreover, as Peter Railton has pointed out, to have many strong desires and be willing to satisfice only at some high level of desire satisfaction is to fail to be moderate in one's desires. In speaking of satisficing moderation, I shall at least for the moment assume the absence of these complicating conditions.

5. Simon, "Theories of Decision Making," p. 264.

6. In fact, it is hard to see how any specific monetary wish can be optimizing if the individual is unsure about his own marginal utility curve for the use of money. And it may well be that we are *necessarily* satisficers in situations where we can wish for whatever we want, unless, perhaps, we are allowed to wish for our own greatest well-being in those very terms. If satisficing were irrational, would that mean that anything other than such an explicitly optimizing wish would be irrational? We shall be discussing some of these issues in Chapter 5.

It has been suggested that the intuitive force of the wish example may depend on the absence of a well-defined upper bound to what one may request. But even if there is no limit to how much money one may request and no such thing as one's greatest possible well-being, one cannot use those facts to explain why it seems to make sense for the person in the example to reject greater heights of well-being for a more moderate level of well-being.

7. Some of these points are made by Philip Pettit in reply to an earlier paper of mine. See his "Satisficing Consequentialism," *Proceedings of the Aristotelian Society*, suppl. 58 (1984), 175.

8. A quite similar point, that the virtuous individual who forgoes something that can only be obtained unjustly need not deny that he is forgoing a good thing, is made in my *Goods and Virtues* (Oxford: Oxford University Press, 1983), chap. 5. On the present view, a person may reasonably turn down the chance of getting more money (say, $90,000) for his house and simply accept what he takes to be a good price (say, $80,000). Does it follow (as Alan Donagan and Jonathan Glover have both suggested) that the moderate individual might (should) turn down a firm $90,000 when $80,000 is on offer? Certainly not. If $80,000 really is a good and sufficient price, then holding out for and striving after a higher amount may seem a form of "grubbing" with little to recommend it. But no such grubbing is involved when the higher price is firmly on offer, and in such a situation nothing need stand in the way of accepting the higher price. Note too that in the normal course of events it will never be clear that that one won't need the extra $10,000, so the case where both $80,000 and $90,000 are firmly on offer is also different from the fairy-tale example where one can wish for enough money to be moderately well off for the rest of one's life and where it is assumed that there will definitely be no need for any more than one is actually wishing for. Once again, there may be reason to take the firm $90,000, even if the moderate individual has no reason to ask for more than moderate wealth in an idealized fairy-tale situation.

9. Compare with Amartya Sen, "Rational Fools: A Critique of the Behavioral Foundations of Economic Theory," *Philosophy and Public Affairs* 6 (1977), *passim*.

10. In *Morals by Agreement* (Oxford: Oxford University Press, 1986), chap. 2, David Gauthier puts forward a pure preference-maximization view of rational choice. He argues for the subjectivity of values and on that basis denies that the content of preferences can be subjected to rational assessment. But he also recognizes that most people are not subjectivists about value and that they are inclined to criticize certain sorts of (consistent, firm, and so forth) preferences as irrational. The view he is proposing is not supposed to be compatible with our ordinary thinking about individualistic rational choice.

11. See Pettit, "Satisficing Consequentialism," p. 172.

12. Similarly, non-egoistic reasons for helping others or doing the honorable thing will not appeal to the egoistic temperament, but this hardly shows that such reasons are illusory. See John McDowell, "The Role of *Eudaimonia* in Aristotle's Ethics," in A. Rorty, ed., *Essays on Aristotle's Ethics* (Berkeley: University of California Press, 1980), pp. 359–376.

13. Davidson's essay is reprinted in his *Essays on Actions and Events*, (Oxford: Oxford University Press, 1980), pp. 21–42. We shall be questioning Davidson's assumptions about weakness of will and irrationality in Chapter 5, below; but for present purposes it is important to see how our account of satisficing moderation can be accommodated to those assumptions.

14. G. E. Moore, *Principia Ethica* (Cambridge: Cambridge University Press, 1959), p. 25.

15. See Samuel Scheffler, *The Rejection of Consequentialism* (Oxford: Oxford University Press, 1982).

16. A similar ambiguity in our usage of "alternative" can similarly lead to confusion and an unwarranted slide from the ascription of moderation to the accusation of incontinence. See Sen, "Rational Fools," pp. 329, 336.

17. Doing enough for others may involve alleviating evils without actually making those others well off; and so it might be supposed that the moral case differs from that of rational satisficing, which is never defensible unless the agent is reasonably well off. But this last assumes that satisficing with respect to discomfort- or pain-alleviation is never rationally acceptable, and it is not clear to me that this is so. Unfortunately, there is no time to pursue this issue of parallelism in all its complexity (see note 4 above).

18. See J. H. Burns and H. L. A. Hart, eds., *An Introduction to the Principles of Morals and Legislation* (New York: Methuen, 1982), p. 12.

19. For a fuller discussion of satisficing consequentialism, see my *Common-Sense Morality and Consequentialism* (Boston: Routledge and Kegan Paul, 1985), chap. 3.

20. However, in strictly consequentialist terms, reconciliation with common sense may not constitute an advantage. See Chapter 8, below.

2. Moderation, Rationality, and Virtue

1. It is also possible, I suppose, for isolated areas of satisficing (optimizing) tendency to exist within a predominantly optimizing (satisficing) personality. Note too that satisficing may be largely a matter of unselfconscious habit, even if the satisficing individual is capable of defending herself with reasons.

2. The notion of "need" at work in satisficing moderation is not basic human need, the requirements of life itself, but some more flexible notion. If someone offers us dinner, we would not ordinarily refuse on the grounds

that, having already had two meals that day, dinner is much more than we need to stay alive and keep functioning. What we take to exceed what we need may therefore be relative to social circumstances and individual background.

3. See John Rawls, *A Theory of Justice* (Cambridge: Harvard University Press, 1971), p. 77; Amartya Sen, "Utilitarianism and Welfarism," *Journal of Philosophy* 76 (1979), 469–470; and Henry Sidgwick, *The Methods of Ethics* (London: Macmillan, 1907), 7th ed., pp. 417, 447.

4. Of course, if one wanted to humor the employee, one might accept the exchange. But it seems perfectly reasonable to reject the exchange and in that case the reason will be as I have said. Also, I am not denying that we sometimes go against the status quo in the name of variety. But where variety is not an issue, as with the present example, the status quo can play a role in motivating our choices.

5. In the text we have focused on two different sorts of reasons for moderate choice; other sorts of reasons may exist, but for the moment I am unable to detect them. It is in any event worth mentioning that the two factors we *have* pointed out bear an eerie analogy to certain scientific-methodological considerations. The methodological desideratum of simplicity involves a preference for explanations that minimize assumed principles or posits, that do not multiply entities beyond necessity. And this clearly resembles the moderate individual's rejection of options that bring her much more than she needs or cares about—indeed, a person who preferred moderate wealth or comfort could be said to have a preference for simplicity in her life. By the same token, methodological conservatism, the theoretical preference for already familiar, satisfactory theories or hypotheses, is strongly reminiscent of the preference for the satisfactory status quo that we find in ordinary practical rationality.

However, I do not want to place any evidentiary weight on these parallels. For one thing, the analogy is quite limited, and there are actually some striking disanalogies between scientific method and satisficing moderation. Not every rational person is moderate in his needs, but it is not clear that scientists differ among themselves in a comparable way in regard to methodological simplicity or conservatism.

6. Both Shelly Kagan and Gregory Trianosky have suggested that the appeal of optimizing/maximizing views of rationality may in part be explainable by our ability to generate them from something like the following attractive, fairly simple set of claims: (1) there is a standing reason to promote one's own good; (2) there are no other extramoral reasons than those mentioned in (1); (3) we are extramorally required to act on the balance of extramoral reasons.

But in fact maximizing/optimizing views fall out only if (1) is strengthened to: (1a) there is a standing reason to promote what is best for oneself. And our whole previous discussion should indicate why (1a) is less compelling than (1). Furthermore, (3) precludes the possibility of rational supererogation, and in Chapter 5 we shall be presenting some arguments in favor of rational supererogation.

7. See my *Goods and Virtues* (Oxford: Oxford University Press, 1983), chap. 2 *passim* and p. 118.

8. On this topic, see *Goods and Virtues*, chap. 6.

9. In emphasizing appearances here and elsewhere, I am not raising epistemological doubts, but rather conveying the assumption that personal traits need to be evaluated at least in part from a social perspective (and from a perspective at least partly external to that imposed by the traits themselves).

10. According to Aristotle and many, many others, a virtuous individual may feel pleasure or satisfaction at having done what virtue requires, even if she was not aiming at such pleasure in acting virtuously. Aristotle sometimes implies that the satisfaction of acting virtuously will always exceed the satisfactions one has to forgo in the name of virtue (see the *Nicomachean Ethics*, 1169a 2–25). But we have absolutely no reason to make this assumption or the more general assumption that the virtuous individual is never required to sacrifice her own well-being or self-interest. (On this see my *Goods and Virtues*, chap. 5.) Similar points apply to satisficing moderation. If what has been said in the text above is on the right track, then a moderate individual may derive a pleased sense of self-sufficiency from satisficing; but in satisficing he is not aiming at this satisfaction, nor is there any reason to assume that the satisfaction involved is always greater than any forgone through satisficing. Satisficing need be no more illusory than self-sacrifice.

11. Michael Bratman has pointed out to me a kind of common-sense self-regarding, non-moral, non-consequentialist reason that does not fit neatly within the structure of such reasons we shall be exploring in Chapter 3 and subsequently, namely: the desire not to vote for oneself in a club election. Some interesting loose ends remain after our discussion.

3. Rational Restrictions on Optimizing

1. To the extent that one may have a debased, bathetic, or niggardly sense of what one needs or when one is comfortably well-off, moderation can drift into asceticism.

2. Aristotle actually uses two terms that can be translated as "moderate." The less frequently used, *metrios*, designates something very close to the common notion of moderation we have been exploring; the other term, *sōphrōn*, represents the major Aristotelian moral virtue mentioned above, a disposition toward the medial with respect to bodily pleasures.

3. In this aspect, common-sense rationality makes its closest approach

to the Aristotelian view, but we have already seen one difference between them and some even more significant differences will emerge later in this chapter.

4. A perfectly good *f* clearly need not be a perfect *f* or the best *f* possible.

5. The restriction more clearly applies to successful efforts to optimize than to the mere acceptance of improvements beyond the point of satisfaction, when the improvements are "thrown into one's lap." For one thing, our common-sense reasons for preferring the status quo come in on the side of keeping what falls into our lap, but work against (or at least do not favor) the effort to optimize beyond what is already (at the point when we act) thoroughly satisfactory.

6. It seems wrongheaded to argue that the mistakes we are talking about are merely mistakes of belief and hence not to be regarded as forms of practical irrationality. The ascetic who acts as if it is best to minimize pleasure, for example, simultaneously embodies a criticizable belief and a criticizable practical attitude or disposition. *Standards* of practical rationality, like moral standards and moral ideals, combine the intellectual with the practical.

7. This is no more plausible than the a priori claim that the warrior who is willing to lay down his life for his country gains a short-run pleasure in being virtuous that (hedonistically) outweighs any future happiness he may have to sacrifice.

8. John Rawls, *A Theory of Justice* (Cambridge: Harvard University Press, 1971), p. 550.

9. See Samuel Scheffler, *The Rejection of Consequentialism* (Oxford: Oxford University Press, 1982), pp. 2, 3, 105, 106.

10. The objectionability of Rule-Utilitarianism is just about the only thing (aside from definitions) that Smart and Williams are in agreement on in their famous debate on the merits of Utilitarianism.

11. See John McDowell's "The Role of *Eudaimonia* in Aristotle's Ethics," in A. Rorty, ed., *Essays on Aristotle's Ethics* (Berkeley: University of California Press, 1980), pp. 359–376.

12. See Aristotle's *Nicomachean Ethics* 1130a 20–22; 1136b 25–1137a 5.

13. In another passage (1118b) Aristotle describes those slavish belly gods who eat to excess and in their self-indulgence eat more than is right. Such people, he says, act culpably and are led to seek the pleasures of food at the cost of everything else. Here we have a moralized critique of excessive devotion to the pleasures of the table alongside a more instrumentalist rational critique of the kind we find in Epicureanism. Again, the possibility of a non-moral, non-instrumentalist rational critique is ignored.

14. Similar points hold *mutatis mutandis* for common-sense strictures against asceticism.

15. See Scheffler, *Rejection,* pp. 84–90.

16. A late famous Speaker of the House once claimed never to have spent a night away from his wife.

17. La Rochefoucauld says that praise of moderation is a way of preventing people from aspiring to greatness. In *The Quest for Certainty* (New York: Minter, Balch, 1919), pp. 280–281, John Dewey mentions that the condemnation of material acquisitiveness is often based on the assumption that such acquisitiveness keeps us from the true ends or higher things of life. But our ordinary sense of the irrationality of an insatiable desire for food or money is not chiefly, or entirely, explainable in these terms. After all, even a fairly "moderate" pursuit of money or good food, which clearly does not seem irrational, may take us away from "higher things" or a "better use" of our time.

4. Rational Restrictions Based on Past History

1. See, for example, Samuel Scheffler, *The Rejection of Consequentialism* (Oxford: Oxford University Press, 1982), pp. 22n, 23n, 85n.

2. To the extent the fickle or inconsistent person creates a disconnection or dissociation between parts of her life, it may be appropriate to bring in Williams's notion of integrity to characterize her *rational* failure. See J. J. C. Smart and B. A. O. Williams, *Utilitarianism: For and Against* (Cambridge: Cambridge University Press, 1973), the contribution by Williams.

3. Notice that if one's life is more unified or consistent as a consequence of choosing to see the Pyramids or keeping a promise, the good involved is not purely internal to one's future, and the optimizing or consequentialistic theory that capitalizes on such goods will therefore lack its usual purely future orientation. Can it too, then, be accused of causal-ancestor worship? Incidentally, I don't believe there is any need for a separate discussion of cases where one has *promised oneself* to do something in the future.

4. See Derek Parfit, *Reasons and Persons* (Oxford: Oxford University Press, 1984), pp. 149–153.

5. I shall not consider (as we did with respect to other reasons in Chapter 2) whether our common-sense reasons not to make capricious changes should be conceived as competitive with reasons of personal good or well-being or as lexically posterior to them (capable only of breaking ties). On either view, there may be situations where some capricious optimizing act is rationally impermissible, but another, non-capricious optimizing act is not rationally excluded. The restriction on optimizing that applies will then have to be understood as ruling out certain ways of optimizing, but not optimizing itself.

6. See John Rawls, *A Theory of Justice* (Cambridge: Harvard University Press, 1971), pp. 426–432.

7. See my *Goods and Virtues* (Oxford: Oxford University Press, 1983), chap. 2 and references.

8. On the distinction between these two kinds or notions of preference-maximizing, see Phillip Bricker, "Prudence," *Journal of Philosophy* 77 (1980), 381–401; see also Parfit, *Reasons and Persons, passim.*

9. Preference-maximizing views lay down conditions of *synchronic* consistency (and transitivity) of preferences, but do not require the kinds of *diachronic* consistency we have been talking about.

10. It might be held that when someone moves from one set of interests and activities to another in an irrational, capricious fashion, it is only the change or transition that is irrational, not the sudden new interests or activities. But in common-sense terms, this distinction seems no better motivated than the parallel idea—which I assume we would want to reject—that when, say, I break my promise to return a book by a certain time, what is wrong is not the failure to return the book, but only my non-returning-of-the-book-having-promised-to-return-it.

In *Change of View* (Cambridge: MIT, 1986), esp. pp. 46, 77, Gilbert Harman comes fairly close to advocating what we have here ascribed to the common-sense view of practical rationality. According to Harman, a principle of conservatism, which tells us to minimize changes in our intentions, is fundamental to practical reason. But his defense of the principle seems to be based more on a desire to draw plausible parallels with theoretical rationality—where Harman believes a principle of conservatism clearly applies—than on any explicit challenge to optimizing or maximizing conceptions of rational choice. Moreover, Harman's principle covers only changes of intention, and we have seen in the present chapter that certain shifts of activity and interest also fall afoul of common-sense restrictions on optimizing/maximizing based on our past history.

However, in his earlier "Practical Reasoning" (*Review of Metaphysics* 29, 1976, 431–463) Harman does consider the broader range of phenomena we have discussed in the present chapter. He points out the existence of a tendency to continue or return to activities and interests out of desire that some part of one's life should not have been "wasted," but he seems more interested in description than in arguing for the operation of a rational principle (constraining optimization) in such cases.

5. *Rational Dilemmas and Rational Supererogation*

1. See, for example, Bernard Williams, "Ethical Consistency," *Problems of the Self* (Cambridge: Cambridge University Press, 1973), chap. 11.

2. See P. R. Foot, "Moral Realism and Moral Dilemma," *Journal of Philosophy* 80 (1983), 394–395.

Notes to Pages 103–111   183

3. Ibid., p. 383.

4. Ruth Marcus, "Moral Dilemmas and Consistency," *Journal of Philosophy* 77 (1980), 125–126.

5. Sophie's choice comes, of course, from William Styron's book by that name, but I believe Patricia Greenspan was the first to bring it into the ongoing debate about moral dilemmas: see her "Moral Dilemmas and Guilt," *Philosophical Studies* 43 (1983), 117–125. I think dilemmas like Sophie's have a special place in discussion of moral dilemmas because of their stark character. In other putative dilemmas, the agent's values are at least clarified or shaped by having to choose between wrongdoings. For example, the young man who came to Sartre determined what kind of person he was by choosing between caring for his infirm mother and joining the Free French. Marcus makes much of the *value-determining* aspect of certain dilemmas, but with Sophie's choice we are clearly faced with a *stark* dilemma: the choice between children is not supposed to determine or clarify Sophie's values.

6. It would be absurd to suppose there are two general principles or obligations involved here: the obligation to care for sons and the obligation to care for daughters, and in any event the example could be reworked so as to involve two daughters. Is anyone going to suggest that we have a general obligation to blonde daughters and another to brunettes? If we were perverse enough, the obligation to keep promises could also be split in two.

7. In my "Utilitarianism, Moral Dilemmas, and Moral Cost," *American Philosophical Quarterly* 22 (1985), 161–168. Some examples of historically possible situations where an agent faces this sort of dilemma are mentioned there, and are briefly discussed in Chapter 7.

8. This topic is discussed at greater length in "Utilitarianism, Moral Dilemmas, and Moral Cost."

9. Though I don't mean to suggest that a guilt so great as to lead to suicide was appropriate for Sophie.

10. One reason for the qualification: Joel Feinberg's well-known example of an agent prevented from making a decision by a coughing fit: perhaps such an agent never had it in his power to act rationally in that particular situation. See Feinberg's "Problematic Responsibility in Law and Morals," in *Doing and Deserving* (Princeton: Princeton University Press, 1970).

11. On certain technical conceptions of preference, the supposition that one uniformly prefers more to fewer happy days may come into conflict with the fact that one inevitably chooses to stand at a distance yielding much fewer extra happy days than some shorter distance that it lay within one's power to choose. If one emphasizes "revealed preference," it is not clear how the preference-maximizing model applies to the fountain-of-youth case or yields a dilemma there. But on some conceptions of preference, the

dilemma seems undeniable, and I shall not enter further into these difficulties, which, in any event, do not affect the dilemmatic character of the example for an optimizing model or common-sense understanding of individualistic rationality. See note 18, below.

12. Indeed, it was chosen for that very reason. Similar examples occurring in the recent philosophic literature raise similar problems about the nature of rationality: see, for example, John Pollock, "How Do You Maximize Expectation Value?" *Noûs* 17 (1984), 409–421; my *Common-Sense Morality and Consequentialism* (Boston: Routledge and Kegan Paul, 1985), pp. 44, 144–145; and my "Utilitarianism, Moral Dilemmas, and Moral Cost," p. 168n. But the previous examples were not used to support the possibility of rational dilemma (indeed Pollock explicitly denies the possibility of dilemma); and in fact those examples may yield dilemmas only if we assume the universal applicability of some optimizing/maximizing model of rationality and deny the rationality of non-instrumental moderation. For some of the examples seem to involve choosing among an infinite number of better and worse results where it doesn't seem to make much difference whether one chooses the better or less good results and where a rational but moderate individual might not care about, be influenced by, such differences in personal good. The examples I have used and will be using here are not naturally thought of in terms of "diminishing returns," and as we shall see, they allow no ready foothold for the idea of non-optimizing moderation. Note further that the infinitistic cases described above are far more problematic for an optimizing/maximizing view than putative cases of rational choice between incommensurable or exactly equal goods. In the latter, one is at least not forced to make a choice that results in *less* good for one than some other choice one could have made.

13. About an additional pleasure or increment of wealth one may say "who needs it," but this is not the response one would expect to an offer of happy, longer life. And "I'm fine as I am" may be a reason for turning down an additional enjoyment, but is irrelevant, of course, to the offer of a longer life.

14. See "The Makropulos Case: Reflections on the Tedium of Immortality," in Williams, *Problems of the Self.*

15. See Donald Davidson, "How is Weakness of the Will Possible?" in J. Feinberg, ed., *Moral Concepts* (Oxford: Oxford University Press, 1969); but see also David Pears, *Motivated Irrationality* (Oxford: Oxford University Press, 1984).

16. The qualification in parentheses rationally permits one to choose between tied-best actions and between incommensurable actions, but still rules out the less-than-best actions described in the text.

17. I cannot think of any other area where "good (not bad) f" entails

"best (available) *f.*" Wouldn't it in fact be odd if this entailment held with respect to good choice and action, but nowhere else?

18. Incidentally, it is not easy for a preference-maximizing view of rationality to make sense of the notion of weakness of will. Very roughly, if actions indicate preferences and preferences determine rationality, then supposedly weak acts will not be irrational, or less rational than certain alternatives. But the idea of "revealed preference" is open to serious objections and a reliance on preferences about preferences may enable us to accommodate the idea of *akrasia*. See David Gauthier, *Morals by Agreement* (Oxford: Oxford University Press, 1986), chap. 2; and Amartya Sen, "Rational Fools: A Critique of the Behavioral Foundations of Economic Theory," *Philosophy and Public Affairs* 6 (1977). By contrast, an individualistically optimizing view of rationality can easily allow for weakness of will, though not, of course, for rational supererogation.

19. Optimizing or maximizing assumptions about rationality lead to problems in the cases Pollock mentions, but in the light of those problems, Pollock goes to the opposite extreme of holding that in the problem cases, anything one does (chooses) is rationally permissible, non-irrational. For reasons already mentioned, this seems an implausible solution for the sorts of cases discussed here (and indeed it seems implausible for Pollock's examples as well, though that implausibility is less obvious if, like Pollock, one doesn't consider questions of degree, what it would be *more* or *less* rational to do). What I am outlining here is a middle path between the view that everything is rationally permissible in our problem cases and the view that they should be treated as dilemmas where no rational choice is possible. This brings them closer to moral life under ordinary assumptions, with impermissible, non-supererogatory permissible, and supererogatory courses of action all available to one.

20. For the interesting application of similar notions to the problem of free will, see Patricia Greenspan's "Unfreedom and Responsibility," in F. Schoeman, ed., *Responsibility, Character, and the Emotions* (Cambridge: Cambridge University Press, 1987). Note that in the fountain-of-youth case it is quite natural to assume that the personal costs of greater efforts are less than the benefits to be gained through greater efforts.

21. The idea of dilemma for such an example could then be resuscitated only if one could make coherent sense of the supposition that (in other possible cases) standing nearer and nearer (without touching) the fountain need not get, or tend to get, more and more difficult.

For interesting explorations of the idea of less-than-ideal *epistemic* rationality see Earl Conee's "Utilitarianism and Rationality," *Analysis* 42 (1982), 55–59; Frederick Kroon, "Rationality and Paradox," *Analysis* 43 (1983), 156–160; Christopher Cherniak, *Minimal Rationality* (Cambridge: MIT, 1986).

6. The Rational Permissions of "Fractional Prudence"

1. See Henry Sidgwick, *The Methods of Ethics*, 7th ed. (London: Macmillan, 1907), pp. 418–419.

2. Compare with S. Scheffler, *The Rejection of Consequentialism* (Oxford: Oxford University Press, 1982), pp. 21–22.

3. See C. I. Lewis, *An Analysis of Knowledge and Valuation* (La Salle, IL: Open Court Press, 1950), pp. 492–493.

4. See Derek Parfit, *Reasons and Persons* (Oxford: Oxford University Press, 1984), pp. 158–186.

5. See J. H. Burns and H. L. A. Hart, eds., *An Introduction to the Principles of Morals and Legislation* (New York: Methuen, 1982), chap. 4.

6. As Shelly Kagan has pointed out to me, this is not entirely fair to Parfit, who allows that different patterns of concern may be *equally* rational. But this still ignores the common-sense view mentioned in the text.

7. We don't need to assume that the fraction required for rationally permissible fractional prudence is the same as that required for morally permissible fractional altruism, nor even that within each of these areas some given fraction has constant validity apart from particular subject matter, circumstances, motivation, or what have you. The idea of fractionality here may be construed either as a placeholder for a more detailed, complex view or as a possibly illuminating metaphor that yields more readily to sensitive intuition than to codification (compare the Aristotelian idea of the mean).

8. See my *Common-Sense Morality and Consequentialism* (Boston: Routledge and Kegan Paul, 1985), chap. 2.

9. Unless they have promised otherwise or have children to raise, and so forth. But I shall ignore the complications.

10. One cannot correctly reply at this point: "But if you were to drop philosophy, you would have different fundamental plans and interests, and your doing so would in fact be justified by the usual considerations of unnecessary sacrifice or integrity." The counterfactual involved here has no justification (see my *Common-Sense Morality*, pp. 20, 140). What we would and should say instead is that it would be irrational for me to drop philosophy, because if I did, it would go against my deepest plans and interests.

11. I have ignored the common-sense moral permission to sacrifice one's own good to the *lesser* good of others, in part because it has no immediately obvious rational analogue and in part because such sacrifice may itself be morally optimal and supererogatory.

7. Rationality-Consequentialism

1. See Henry Sidgwick, *The Methods of Ethics*, 7th ed. (London: Macmillan, 1907), p. 11.

2. See Samuel Scheffler, *The Rejection of Consequentialism* (Oxford: Oxford University Press, 1982), chap. 1; and Amartya Sen, "Evaluator Relativity and Consequentialist Evaluation," *Philosophy and Public Affairs* 12 (1983), 113–132.

3. The instrumentalist, two-tiered conception of rational moderation discussed in Chapter 3 can be described as a form of *indirect* rationality-consequentialism, but in the present chapter we shall be limiting our discussion to forms of direct rationality-consequentialism.

4. See Sidgwick's *Methods*, pp. 497–498.

5. Ibid., pp. 497–498, 507.

6. Ibid., p. 411.

7. Ibid., p. 208.

8. See John Rawls, *A Theory of Justice* (Cambridge: Harvard University Press, 1971), pp. 26–27.

9. On this point see Rawls, *Theory of Justice*, sects. 5 and 30 (however, contrast p. 182); Thomas Nagel, "Subjective and Objective," in his *Mortal Questions* (Cambridge: Cambridge University Press, 1979), esp. pp. 202–204; Nagel, "The Limits of Objectivity," in S. McMurrin, ed., *The Tanner Lectures on Human Values*, vol. 1 (Cambridge: Cambridge University Press, 1980), pp. 117–139; and Peter Railton, "Moral Realism," *Philosophical Review* 95 (1986), 163–207.

10. The view that actual results are what count does not lead to the absurd conclusion that accidental occurrences such as slipping on a banana peel qualify as rational or irrational depending on their actual consequences. Rationality characterizations apply to choices and intentional actions (and appropriately related habits or dispositions of choice and action); and purely accidental occurrences involving humans need not, therefore, count as either rational or irrational. Utilitarian consequentialism guards itself against similar absurdities by restricting its characterizations to intentional actions (and motives, intentions, and dispositions appropriately related to such actions).

11. See Karl Popper's *The Open Society and Its Enemies* (London: Routledge and Kegan Paul, 1974), I, chap. 5, n. 6; chap. 9, n. 2.

12. A much fuller treatment of this and related issues occurs in my "Utilitarianism, Moral Dilemmas, and Moral Cost," *American Philosophical Quarterly* 22 (1985), 161–168.

13. Some possible further conditions, hinted at here and in Chapter 5 above, are discussed at greater length in "Utilitarianism, Moral Dilemmas, and Moral Cost."

14. See my *Common-Sense Morality and Consequentialism* (Boston: Routledge and Kegan Paul, 1985), chap. 5.

15. In "Moral Realism," Railton seems to put a greater emphasis on comparative judgments of rationality and morality than on positive judg-

ments of rationality and morality, but he never rules out the possibility of making the latter objectively. The more one relies on comparative judgments, however, the readier one may be to discard positive judgments altogether and the more willing, perhaps, to accept an explicitly scalar view.

8. Implications for Ethics

1. Optimizing, satisficing, and scalar views of rational choice can focus either on personal good or solely on the satisfaction of self-regarding or extramoral preferences. If we insist on substantial analogy between the moral and rational parts of what we are calling total views, then any form of rationality-consequentialism that concerns itself with preference satisfaction and makes no claims about personal good will have a moral analogue that concerns itself exclusively with preferences. Thus, for example, the moral analogue of the view that extramoral rationality consists in maximizing the (expectable) satisfaction of the agent's self-regarding preferences will wish to say that morally right choices and acts maximize the (expectable) satisfaction of all preferences, but will not tie such preference satisfaction to any notion of social/impersonal or, presumably, personal good. Such a moral analogue will in that case not count as a form of (utilitarian) act-consequentialism in the usual sense, and will in fact be a rather unfamiliar kind of moral view. Act-consequentialism relates rightness to resulting good states of affairs and human good, but the moral view just mentioned— and any other strictly analogous to an exclusively preference-oriented account of rationality—doesn't say that the chosen act that maximizes the expectable satisfaction of all preferences has impersonally or personally better consequences than any alternative: it has nothing at all to say about good consequences. So it is worth noting that preference for a purely preference-oriented view of rationality and the natural desire for analogy between morality and rationality leads— perhaps surprisingly—to an essentially unfamiliar—"bizarre" may not be too strong a word—moral view that is far from standard (utilitarian) consequentialism. (The "preference utilitarianism" of John Harsanyi focuses on the individual's "true" preferences and relates these to what is "really good" for an individual. Social utility is likewise understood as what makes a society "better off." So views like Harsanyi's are not what I am criticizing here. See his "Morality and the Theory of Rational Behavior" in Amartya Sen and Bernard Williams, eds., *Utilitarianism and Beyond* (Cambridge, England: Cambridge University Press, 1982), pp. 39–62, esp. p. 56.

I think we need to be wary of purely preference-oriented moral views and to resist purely preference-oriented accounts of individual rationality, if we are inclined to think in terms of analogies between morality and extramoral rationality. (Of course, this argument is more likely to appeal to philosophers than to economists.) And in any event, we can now see further reason for having organized the present book around the analogous ways in which common-sense rationality and common-sense morality contrast, respectively, with optimizing rationality and optimizing act-consequentialism. To have chosen pure preference-maximizing views as moral and rational baselines would have involved us with a view of right action that is philosophically aberrant. And it seemed better to take off from more familiar and widely accepted views in our attempt to ground rational commonsensism by analogy with moral commonsensism.

2. See John Rawls, *A Theory of Justice* (Cambridge: Harvard University Press, 1971), pp. 22–27.

3. See Derek Parfit, "Later Selves and Moral Principles," in Alan Montefiore, ed., *Philosophy and Personal Relations* (London: Routledge and Kegan Paul, 1973), pp. 137–169.

Index